The Greatest Civilizations of the Americas: The History and Culture of the Maya, Aztec, and Inca

By Charles River Editors

Introduction

Mayapan

Many ancient civilizations have influenced and inspired people in the 21st century. The Greeks and Romans continue to fascinate the West today. But of all the world's civilizations, none have intrigued people more than the Mayans, whose culture, astronomy, language, and mysterious disappearance all continue to captivate people.

In 2012 especially, there has been a renewed focus on the Mayans, whose advanced calendar has led many to speculate the world will end on the same date the Mayan calendar ends. The focus on the "doomsday" scenario, however, has overshadowed the Mayans' true contribution to astronomy, language, sports, and art.

The Greatest Civilizations of the Americas discusses the Mayan calendar within the larger context of their astronomical advances, while also providing a comprehensive analysis of their history, empire, and culture. Along with a description of Mayan life and pictures of Mayan ruins and art, the mystique of the Maya is traced from the height of their empire to the present day, in an attempt to understand a civilization often been best described as an enigma.

Aztec Dancers, San Miguel de Allende. Photo: Alan McNairn

From the moment Spanish conquistador Hernan Cortes first found and confronted them, the Aztecs have fascinated the world, and they continue to hold a unique place both culturally and in pop culture. Nearly 500 years after the Spanish conquered their mighty empire, the Aztecs are often remembered today for their major capital, Tenochtitlan, as well as being fierce conquerors of the Valley of Mexico who often engaged in human sacrifice rituals.

Ironically, and unlike the Mayans, the Aztecs are not widely viewed or remembered with nuance, in part because their own leader burned extant Aztec writings and rewrote a mythologized history explaining his empire's dominance less than a century before the Spanish arrived. Naturally, Cortes and other Spaniards depicted the Aztecs as savages greatly in need of conversion to Catholicism. While the Mayans are remembered for their astronomy, numeral system, and calendar, the Aztecs have primarily been remembered in a far narrower way, despite continuing to be a source of pride to Mexicans through the centuries.

As a result, even though the Aztecs continue to interest people across the world centuries after their demise, it has fallen on archaeologists and historians to try to determine the actual history, culture, and lives of the Aztecs from the beginning to the end, relying on excavations, primary accounts, and more. *The Greatest Civilizations of the Americas* looks at this whole story, in an attempt to portray the Aztecs as they actually were. Along with pictures of Aztec art and ruins, this book describes the Aztecs' lives, religion, art, cities, and empire, in an attempt to better understand the once dominant civilization.

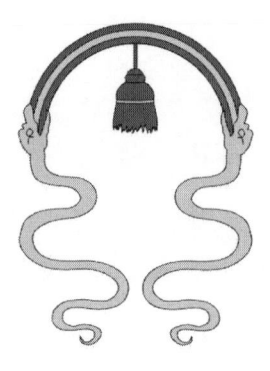

Banner of the Inca

During the Age of Exploration, Native American tribes fell victim to European conquerors seeking legendary cities made of gold and other riches, attempts that were often being made in vain. And yet, of all the empires that were conquered across the continent, the one that continues to be most intimately associated with legends of gold and hidden riches is the Inca Empire. The Inca Empire, which flourished in modern day Peru and along the west coast of South America, was the largest Native American empire in pre-Columbian America until Pizarro and the Spanish conquistadors conquered them in the 16th century. What ultimately sealed their doom was the rumor that huge amounts of gold were available in regions south of the Andes Mountains.

Though the Spanish physically conquered them in quick fashion, the culture and legacy of the Inca Empire has continued to endure throughout the centuries in both Europe and South America, due in no small part to the fact they were one of the most advanced and sophisticated cultures on the continent. Like the Aztecs, the Spanish burned much of the Inca's extant writings, but it is estimated that as many as 35 million once fell under their banner, and the empire's administrative skills were so sharp that they kept accurate census records. Their religion, organization, and laws were also effectively centralized and tied to the rulers of the empire, and their military mobilization would have made the ancient Spartans proud. After the Spanish conquest, several rebellions in the area attempted to reestablish the proud Inca Empire over the next two centuries, all while famous Europeans like Voltaire glorified the Inca Empire in optimistic artistic portrayals.

The mystique and aura of the Inca continue to fascinate the world today, and nowhere is this more prominent than at Macchu Picchu, which was "lost" for over 300 years and remains the subject of intense debate among historians. The magnificent ruins and the inability of historians to crack the code used for the Inca's few surviving written records all continue to add to the mystery and interest in the Inca civilization.

The Greatest Civilizations of the Americas comprehensively covers the culture and history of pre-Columbian America's largest empire. Along with pictures of Inca art, clothing and ruins, this book describes the Inca's lives, religion, cities, and empire, in an attempt to better understand the once dominant but still mysterious civilization.

The Maya

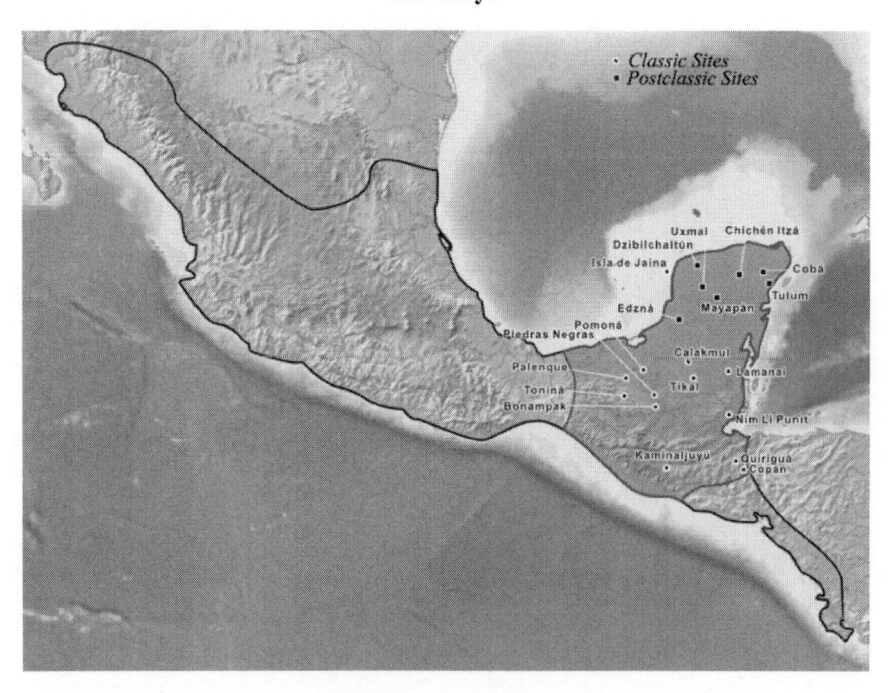

Map of the Mayan Empire

Chapter 1: The Enigma of the Maya

Depiction of Upakal K'inich in Palenque

Ubiquitous in popular and scholarly descriptions of Maya civilization is the word enigma. In spite of tremendous advances in archaeology that continue to reveal more and more information on the highly developed Maya civilization of Mesoamerica, there remain many unanswered questions. Two examples of significant unresolved questions concerning the Maya illustrate the serious holes in our knowledge. Despite the existence of their civilization in South America for thousands of years, historians and archaeologists still cannot explain where the Maya came from or exactly why their civilization collapsed.

Why have these questions continued to go unanswered? These unsolved mysteries surrounding the Maya civilization persist in large measure due to the efficiency of the Spanish in eradicating the remnants of Maya culture. And unlike the Aztecs, the disappearance of the Mayans cannot be clearly traced to a series of battles. By the early 16th century the Spanish conquistadors, along with the colonists and zealous propagators of the faith who followed the likes of Cortes and Pizarro, set out to systematically destroy the indigenous Maya civilization of the Yucatan that was already in decline even before their arrival. The land-grabbing colonists used the natives as virtual slave labor and pillaged their cities, while enthusiastic Catholic baptizers did their best to erase their heathen beliefs.

While the blame for the loss of much of the Mayan culture can be heaped upon the Spanish, much of what is known about life in a Maya community comes from the writings of the Provincial of the Franciscans in the Yucatan, Bishop Diego de Landa. His 1566 book, *Relación de las cosas de Yucatán* (An Account of the Affairs in the Yucatan), contains detailed observations on the culture of the Maya, including a record of their hieroglyphics and writing system. These have proved to be invaluable sources for those piecing together a picture of Mayan life. But Bishop Landa was also responsible for what in retrospect was an incalculable loss for the world. The Mayans' developed the only full language during the Mesoamerican period, but Landa and his Franciscan cohorts confiscated a great number of books written in the Mayan language which they believed were full of heretical ideas and burned them all. Bishop Landa's well-intentioned bonfire of books left the world with only four extant Maya manuscripts and a 1558 record written in Latin characters of Maya cosmology called the *Popol Vuh*, or book of the people preserving oral tradition of the K'iche Maya of Guatemala.

The Maya's writings obviously weren't the only things lost to history. In the years after the conquest of the Maya some of their cities were mined by the colonists for building materials. A spectacular example of this is took place at Izamal, where Bishop Landa's Monastery of San Antonio de Padua was constructed with stones reused from a Maya building. The Monastery itself, rising above the colonial town, sits on a plinth that is, in fact, a truncated Maya pyramid. Other Maya cities still inhabited in the period of conquest were abandoned and eventually obscured by jungle vegetation. Explorers in the jungle still find lost ruins of the Maya in Central America, and one incorrect story that made the rounds in 2011 speculated that Mayan ruins were found in North Georgia, a reflection of the interest and uncertainty still surrounding the Maya.

In the early 19th century, explorers and adventurers began to rediscover several Maya sites. Following the opinions of the colonists. who at the time perceived the contemporary Maya as unsophisticated and culturally impoverished, the explorers were initially convinced that these people could not have been responsible for such elaborate building projects. Given some of their similarities to the ancient civilizations in Europe and Egypt, they concluded that the Maya pyramids and other structures they discovered must have somehow been the work of Greeks, Romans, Egyptians or Indians from India. How exactly these American city builders got to the region was explained by fanciful conjecture on cultural migration.

In the middle of the 19th century, John Lloyd Stephens and the topographical artist Frederick Catherwood systematically explored the Mayan ruins of British Honduras, Guatemala and the Yucatan. The subsequent publication of Stephens' description of the Maya ruins and Catherwood's illustrations in *Incidents of Travel in Central America, Chiapas, and the Yucatán* in 1841 and *Incidents of Travel in Yucatán* in 1843 were best sellers. They were also responsible for an upsurge in interest in the mysteries of lost civilizations. In the last half of the 19th century, a number of other explorers recorded Maya sites, and in 1881, English archaeologist Alfred Maudslay began the first modern scientific study of a number of Maya cities. His work inspired American archaeologists associated with Harvard University to undertake expeditions, and these in turn were followed by many university and museum sponsored digs right up to the present day. Interest in the Maya began an upswing that carries through today.

The many (and ongoing) accounts of discoveries of Mayan cities by archaeologists and explorers have only added to the mysteries of the Maya civilization, which in turn continue to fuel interest and speculation. Early archaeologists attributed names to the buildings in many sites based on assumptions as to their use, which has led to misleading descriptions that should be paid little attention. At Uxmal, today a very popular Yucatan tourist destination, there are buildings called the Nunnery and the Governor's Palace, both of which are based on quite fanciful ideas of the original purpose of the structures. At Chichén Itzá, the greatest Maya city in the Yucatan, one is taken by guides to a building called the Nunnery for no good reason other than the small rooms reminded the Spaniards of a nunnery back home. Similarly the great pyramid at Chichén Itzá is designated the El Castillo, the Castle, which it certainly is not, and the Observatory is called El Caracol, the Snail, for its spiral staircase. This kind of confusing naming of Maya structures had been abandoned at recently discovered sites and replaced with less colorful terms such as, for example, Temple 1, Temple II and so on at Tikal in Guatemala.

The Pyramid of the Magician at Uxmal and Building of the Iguana at Uxmal are perfect examples of fanciful but nonsensical names

The Castle at Chichén Itzá

Chapter 2: The Origins and Spreading of the Maya Civilization

Today the Aztecs are remembered as the civilization with the vast South American empire, but the Mayans spread across a wide swath of land themselves. The region of Mesoamerica inhabited by the Maya stretched from the dry, flat limestone plains of the Yucatan to the wet, mountainous jungle of Chiapas and Guatemala and on to the narrow flatland of the Pacific coast. The first inhabitants of the region are believed to have been hunter gatherers, and anthropologists think these primitive people were descended from the early migrants who moved from Asia across to the northern reaches of North America and spread south around 14,000 B.C. Once settled, a more agricultural society developed in central Mexico in the fifth millennium BCE. These people were able to reliably grow crops of corn, beans and squashes through slash and burn field preparation, but depending on the quantity and quality of the soil, a field had a limited life expectancy. In some regions, particularly those where the soil cover was thin and the rainfall limited, the slash and burn technique of crop cultivation required careful attention to the seasonal weather pattern.

Around 1800 B.C., the Olmecs, the earliest traceable civilization of Mesoamerica, built cities that depended on reliable agricultural production. Many details of Olmec society remain a mystery, but it is known that some of their practices, such as building pyramids and playing a ritual ball-game, were similar to those of the later Maya. Nevertheless, the precise relationship between the Olmec and the Maya culture is as yet unknown. What is known is that while the earliest Maya communities on the Pacific coast and in the Guatemalan highlands and Belize were on the rise, the Olmec civilization, with its population centers near the region of modern Veracruz and Villahermosa in Mexico, was in decline.

The history of the Maya is divided into periods that have been given names and dates that are not currently unanimously accepted. The nomenclature of the chronology of Maya civilization was created by Eurocentric scholars who held fixed ideas on the rise, flourishing and decline of civilizations, in keeping with the tracking of the Greek and Roman empires of antiquity. In particular, readers should be cautious of the word classic, as it implies a superior rank or model or standard which does not really apply to the evolution of Maya culture. Still, this chronology, even with its imperfections, does allow for a quick survey of the evolution of Maya civilization.

The Early Preclassic period dating from 1800 to 900 B.C. is the era when the Olmecs established their major cities at Paso de la Amada in Chiapas and San Lorenzo in southern Veracruz. In the Middle Preclassic Period, spanning the years from 900 to 300 B.C., the first Maya cities were built on the Pacific coast, in places like Itzapa near Tapachula, in the Guatemalan highlands at such sites as Kaminaljuyú now underneath Guatemala City, and the recently excavated mega-city El Mirador. It is currently held that Maya city building expanded north further into the Guatemalan Highlands and Belize.

Pyramid at El Mirador

It was in the Late Preclassic Period from 300 B.C.-250 A.D. that archaeologists believe Maya culture developed a high level of complexity. This included the appearance of writing in the Mayan language and a sophisticated continuing calendar system. In the Early Classic Period, 250-600 A.D., Maya civilization flourished, particularly in the city of Tikal in modern

Guatemala. Major construction was carried out at Copán in modern Honduras and at Palenque in Chiapas, Mexico. The period Late Classic, 600-950 A.D., is used by Mayanists to designate the age in which civilization reached its height. This was the time when the great cities of the Yucatan or northern lowlands flourished and the cities of the southern lowlands declined. It was also late in this period that the city of Chichén Itzá rose to prominence.

The Main Plaza at Tikal

The final period in the chronology used by scholars of Maya civilization is the Post Classic Period 950-1530 A.D. which saw the collapse of Chichén Itzá and the rise of Mayapán, the last leading city of Maya culture. The four surviving Mayan codices were written during this period.

Given the manner in which Maya cities flourished in different periods and were built in different environments, from the lush jungle in the south to the wet coastlands of Belize and the dry limestone plains of the Yucatan, it is not surprising that the Maya were not a homogenous people. In different regions of their empire, Mayan people and cities had distinctly different economies, social organization, art and architecture. Variation existed over time and geography. It is important to keep that in mind when discussing Mayan culture.

Chapter 3: Life in a Maya City

Social Status

Mayan panel depicting King T'ah 'Ak' Cha'an

Maya civic society in its fully developed form was organized around a king or *ahau*, from whose lineage his successors were chosen. The king or lord was the embodiment of religious life in the city, and for that he was assisted by noble warriors, the *sahalob*. The Maya believed that the well-being of the rest of the community depended on the religious rituals performed by the royal court, so the community supported the *ahau* and his clan with voluntary offerings of food and labor. The former would have been particularly burdensome in years of drought in the northern lowlands, and the latter must have been exceedingly taxing considering how much stone and rubble was transported in the process of building pyramids, palaces, temples and roads.

Not every contribution was voluntary, however. The king not only received levies from the inhabitants of his city, but he also, in some cases, required that vassal cities and communities render him tribute. The wealth of a king and his court was thus directly dependent on how many vassal states he had and the population of his own city. The king and his clan of aristocrats consequently lived better than everyone else and enjoyed an abundance of luxuries provided as tribute or through trading the excess of this "in kind" payment with neighboring cities. In this way jade, amber and obsidian, cotton, cacao, honey and salt were available to the principal kings and their courts.

Based on depictions in sculpture and wall paintings in the Classic Period, the Maya kings, presumably only on formal occasions, sported large headdresses that were held up by racks attached to their backs. These wooden decorations were painted and enriched with shells, jade, feathers and textiles and sometimes an image of Chaac, the rain god, or Ahau Kin, the sun god. The nose, which was a particularly important element in the Maya concept of beauty, would be built up with putty. To obtain a nose with a profile that was a continuation of the slope of the forehead, aristocratic Mayans bound an infant's head with a board to control its shape. The ears of the kings and aristocrats were decorated with elaborate ornaments attached to enlarged lobes, and their teeth were carefully filed and filled with inlays of jade. The king had a wardrobe of formal costumes so that he appeared in garb appropriate to his functions as priest, war lord, or presiding official at ball games.

The power and central importance of a king in Maya culture is illustrated in the impressive memorial structure built by King Pakal at Palenque in Mexico. Several years before his death at the age of 81 in 684 A.D. Pakal had a 27 meter pyramid constructed against a natural hill. His nine level pyramid with a steep narrow stairway running up the front is topped by a temple with five entrances. On the pillars between the entrances are inscriptions recording the royal lineage of Pakal. From the Temple of Inscriptions, a stairway leads down into the bowels of the pyramid to a burial crypt. Here King Pakal's body, decorated with jade necklaces and wearing a face mask of jade obsidian and shells, was entombed in a painted sarcophagus. On the lid of the sarcophagus was carved an image of Pakal descending the world-tree into the underworld. When the crypt was discovered in 1951, it contained the skeletons of four malew and one female. It is assumed that the bones are the remains of captives sacrificed to accompany Pakal to the underworld.
King Pakal himself began the building of his tomb. It was completed during the reign of his son Kan-Balam II who recorded his contribution by having a stucco panel installed in the Temple of Inscriptions showing him as a baby in his father's arms.

The society of the Maya was stratified. The king who owed his position to a royal lineage was surrounded by nobles that obtained their rank through paternal descent, although their status was even higher if they were also descended from nobility on the maternal side. Among the nobility in some Maya cities were prosperous farmers, successful merchants, priests and warriors. The duties of the court included maintaining civic order, recording the history of the community in sculpture and inscriptions, keeping the calendar, recording astronomical information and divining the future from it, and managing war and trade. Below the nobility were the free workers who were allocated a *hun* or *uinic* of 400 square feet of land to farm. They paid an in-kind levy to the king and temple priests, who would divine ideal times for planting and harvest. The Mayans strongly that neither good things nor bad things occurred by chance, which is why they were so bent on studying the patterns of the sun and stars. They believed these patterns were set in motion by the gods to help the Maya reveal their divine intentions.

In addition to Maya inscriptions and sculpture that have now been deciphered, information on life in a Maya city was recorded by Bishop Diego de Landa in his *Relación*. As a Christian European, he was fascinated with the Maya system of justice. In particular, he recorded the various crimes that involved a punishment of execution and public humiliation. One of the details he included in his account was the punishment for adultery. The guilty party would be punished by having his head crushed by a rock thrown by the offended husband. For lesser crimes such as theft, the culprit was put into temporary slavery. This would be humiliating to the Mayans, because the permanent slaves in a typical Maya community were low level captives of war. The more prestigious captives of war were "luckier." These prestigious enemy warriors were spared a life of slavery and were apparently treated well until they were required for ritual sacrifice.

Food and Farming

The vast majority of the population of Maya cities consisted of farmers, who mostly lived in wood-framed reed huts on an elevated platform, much like those that can be seen today in rural Mayan communities in the Yucatan. This was sensible, since a high level of food production was necessary to sustain populations that were quite astonishing in size. In the Late Classic period around 600 A.D., the city of Tikal in Guatemala is estimated to have had a population of 39,000 people, with another 10,000 living in the hinterland around the city. At its peak, Palenque had about 6,000 inhabitants, Uxmal had perhaps 15,000, and Chichén Itzá may have had over 30,000 inhabitants. With different features and climates, the methods and successes of farming around these various communities were not always similar. In the northern lowlands, cities such as Uxmal and Chichén Itzá had precarious food supplies that depended, in part, on slash and burn agriculture. In the farthest reaches of the southern lowlands, at cities like Palenque, water was plentiful and reliable crop production was the norm. Here, because the depth of the soil was significantly more than that of the northern lowlands, cleared land could be productive for 10 years or longer.

Mayan farms produced a variety of crops, the staples being corn or maize with beans and squashes. In some Maya communities, cotton, cocoa and honey were produced, and whatever wasn't used for basic living was traded. Along the coast of modern Belize, Maya agricultural practices included the use of irrigation ditches, mounded fields and reclamation of swamp land. These techniques would have ensured a very long period of productivity for agriculture.

Depending on the location of their community, the Mayans typically ate animals that they hunted, and along the shore in the Yucatan at maritime trading cities like Cozumel and Tulum, and in Belize, the Maya had a diet that included quantities of fish.

Warfare

It is a commonly held belief among scholars that warfare between Maya cities erupted when there was a shortage of food, either because of drought or insufficient production to support an expanding population. Although there is no direct evidence, it is supposed that one city would expand into the territory of another and there would be competition for land.

Most of the theories on Maya warfare are based on two fairly inadequate assumptions. One is that all Maya city populations were identical over the entire history of the civilization, and the other is that Maya behaved like Europeans. Instead, some scholars now believe that some Maya cities engaged in ferocious warfare from time to time, while others were involved in only occasional skirmishes with their neighbors. In piecing together the evidence of Maya culture it is necessary to remember that the Maya civilization of interest to archaeologists existed between 900 B.C.-1200 A.D., and that their cities were scattered in the huge territory lying between the Pacific coast of Guatemala and the northern reaches of the Yucatan peninsula. To assume that Maya culture was monolithic and consistent is a holdover from colonial beliefs in the simplicity of the indigenous people they conquered.

While it has historically been the Aztecs who were viewed as a militaristic civilization, there is considerable debate among scholars on the question of territorial aggression among the Maya. Because many of the Maya cities lack fortifications that are like those Eurocentric archaeologists might have expected, it was once assumed that the Maya created for themselves an ideal, pacifistic society. But others have considered the Maya as particularly ferocious in warfare, taking captives for ritual sacrifice and appropriating territories through force. Still others have explained the demise of certain Maya cities by arguing that they were devastated by internecine warfare that doomed both sides of the fighting. As with many aspects of Maya society, the presence or absence of bellicose behavior is an enigma. There have been some findings of parapets and ramparts, in particular at Tikal and Becán, clear proof that the Mayans saw the need for defensive fortifications for those cities. But the fact that such ramparts were not a consistent part of Maya city construction is evidence that there was considerable variation in aggression, expansion and cooperation from one city to another.

Chapter 4: The Myths and Religion of the Maya

The Spanish, along with other modern explorers and anthropologists named Mayan buildings strange names because they didn't understand their use. Thus it is not surprising the religious beliefs of the Maya are also not always clear from the remaining structures and art among their ruins. It is assumed that the buildings archaeologists have called temples and the pyramids found in the centre of Maya cities were the sites of religious rituals, but exactly what these rituals consisted of is a matter of conjecture.

What is known about the beliefs of the Maya comes primarily from the *Popol Vuh*, a compendium of oral tradition among Guatemalan K'iche Maya. This book, written by a Maya in the 18th century, tells the story of the creation of the earth. It is through a synopsis of the creation myth that people today can get a glimpse of some of the major features of Maya society, including their relationship with the land, the importance of family connections, the duality of the gods, and the central role of corn in the life of the Maya.

In the tradition of the K'iche Maya, the vast flat earth lies between 13 levels of heaven rising above and nine layers of underworld below. At the four corners of the world, trees, or according to some, giants (*bacabs*), hold up the heaven. At the centre of the world a great tree connected the earth, heaven and the underworld.

Before the creation of the world there was only sky and water. In the water lived the god Gucumatz or Sovereign Plumed Serpent, and in the heavens dwelt the god Huracán or Heart of the Sky. The sky god and the sea god met and conversed, and their discourse or debate brought life into being. It is interesting that the Maya, who seem to have been particularly enlightened on the subject, should consider that it took two gods to create the world and its inhabitants, and that cooperative gods accomplished this task through rational conversation. Gucumatz and Huracán talked about the earth, and this caused the waters to part. The earth rose up, mountains appeared and forests, lakes and streams formed. From their dialogue on what life should populate the earth animals were created.

Sculptured depiction of Gucumatz

Like many gods in ancient mythology in America, Europe and Asia, Huracán and Gucumatz manifest themselves in other guises. Huracán, a one-legged god, is associated with Tahil, Obsidian Mirror or Torch Mirror, who appears in sculpture at Palenque. The god Gucumatz is a manifestation of the serpent feather deity Quetzalcóatl or, as he was called by the Yucatec Maya, Kukulcán. The story of the beginnings of the earth involves a paradox. On the one hand

Gucamatz and Huracán are considered as unique and singular gods, but on the other hand they are said to have belonged to groups of sky and sea gods. This kind of paradox is not unusual in creation myths,

The various animals created to inhabit appropriate environments in the world could not speak. They were thus unable to honor the gods as Gucumatz and Huracán wished. The co-creators discussed the problem and agreed to create man. At first they tried to model man from mud but when it rained he disintegrated. Then they tried to form him from wood. But the wooden people they created had empty hearts. The wooden Maya also had a tendency to warp. The failure of the second attempt at the creation of humans led the gods to create a flood to destroy them. The animals and, interestingly, the already created stone maize grinders, rose up and killed all but a few of the remaining wooden creatures. A few escaped death and the gods allowed them to live as monkeys, but they were unable to praise the gods.

It was in the era of wooden people when there was neither day nor night but only perpetual dusk that the god Seven Macaw, who saw himself as the great creator, boasted of his importance. He claimed that his eyes framed in metal and his teeth encrusted with jewels along with his shiny nose were the sun, moon and sky. The twin sons of the god Hun Hunahpú and Blood Moon, a maiden of the underworld, attacked the upstart Seven Macaw. One of the Hero Twins, Hunahpú shot Seven Macaw, breaking his jaw, but in the struggle Seven Macaw detached Hunahpú 's arm. The twins appealed to their grandfather, Great White Peccary, and grandmother, Great White Tapir, for help. The grandparents persuaded Seven Macaw that his toothache, really his broken jaw, was caused by worms gnawing in his mouth. They volunteered to extract Seven Macaw's jewel encrusted teeth, and instead of replacing them with bone ones they installed kernels of corn in his mouth. They also removed the metal decorations around his eyes. Stripped of his finery Seven Macaw lost his powers and expired, and Hunahpú happily retrieved his arm.

After the relation of the story of Seven Macaw, the *Popol Vuh* continues the tale of the creation of man by Huracán and Gucumatz. Their failure to create man from either mud or wood did not discourage them. They next tried creating mankind from maize or corn, which, of course, was to be staples of life for the Maya. The creator gods took maize to a grandmother goddess, Xmucané, who created a maize paste with which the gods could make human flesh. They squeezed out some of the water from the tortilla base, in our terms a kind of soup of stem cells, and used it to make blood. They created four males from the tortilla flour and blood, and these first four males became the founding fathers of the four K'iche clans. These humans were not only capable of work and of praising the creators, but they were endowed with acute hearing and precise vision. So good were their ears and eyes that they could discern even the hidden meaning of things. The gods, upset at this intrusive talent, decided to dim the human faculties. The perfected male humans were soon joined by women who were given senses that, like their male companions, were less acute than those of the gods.

In addition to the *Popol Vuh*, other texts have assisted archaeologists and ethnologists in their quest to understand Maya religion. Written in Mayan and transcribed in Latin script in the late 18th or early 19th century, the *Books of Chilam Balam* record the memories of pre-conquest society, in this case, in some Yucatecan towns.

Chapter 5: Unique Features of Maya Civilization

The Maya Calendar

In 2012, much of the interest in the Maya is a result of their calendar, particularly the fact that it ends on December 21, 2012. While many incorrectly presume that the Maya were predicting the world to end on that date, it is not a coincidence that their calendar ended on the winter solstice. The Maya developed a sophisticated method of calculating and creating a calendar that is astonishing even by today's standards, and their advancements in applied mathematics not only has intrigued archaeologists but has been incorporated into the beliefs of New Agers and modern apocalyptic doomsayers. In the history of arithmetic, their use of zero stands as a milestone of great significance, which placed them ahead of contemporary Europeans. In Europe, this essential concept was not part of the canon of calculation until the Renaissance.

Mayan numerology

The Maya numerical system was based on units of 20. To represent the numerals 1 to 4 they used dots. Five was written with a horizontal bar and 6 was a bar with a dot above. Up to 19, the

Maya were able to use a system of dots and bars. For example three bars and a dot signified 16. The zero was represented by a shell. The written number system not only allowed calculation of items of trade but also permitted the calculations necessary in order to record time, as well as for the creation of a calendar.

The Maya used two calendars. One was a 260 day ritual calendar with twelve 20 day cycles. They also used a 365 solar count calendar which consisted of eighteen months of 20 days, and five uncategorized days at the end of the year. While this calendrical system was common in Mesoamerican cultures, the Maya were unique in the creation of what is called the Long Count. They established a zero date which has been correlated with the West's Gregorian calendar to stand for August 11, 3114 B.C. Time was measured from this starting date in five units, a *baktun* of 144,000 days, a *katun* of 7,200 days, a *tun* of 360 days, a *uinal* of 20 days, and a *kin* of 1 day. Dates were written with a point between each unit so that a date from year zero would be so many *baktuns* followed by a dot, then so many *katuns* followed by a dot, so many *tuns* and so on. Using this Long Count method of indicating dates, the Maya recorded in inscriptions and on freestanding commemorative relief carved stones (stelae) the actual date of important events, such as the accession of a king or a military victory. In Maya civilization time was an essential concept. The past, the present and the future were clearly related and all kinds of social activities could be managed in a world organized by time.

For day to day purposes the Maya used the ritual calendar of twelve 20 day cycles. Each month was given a name and astrologers using the celestial bodies could plot the most auspicious time for such activities as planting or waging war. A priest scribe, *ak k'u hun* ("servant of the sun"), managed the connection between astronomy and the calendar, and as keeper of the time he was also the curator of the genealogies of kings and nobles.

With its 225 day orbit around the sun and its phases, Venus was one focus of astronomical observation from observatories like the one at Chichén Itzá. To the Maya, the cyclical disappearance of Venus connected the planet with the underworld. The appearance of Venus as the morning star and evening star were predicted by Maya astronomers with an accuracy of one day in 6,000 years. The observatory at Chichén Itzá (the Coracol) was built primarily for the observation of Venus, and the three doors to the inner chamber line up with precisely with the position in the western sky where Venus can be seen as the evening star. Evidence of the importance of astronomical prediction in Maya society is found in two of the surviving Maya manuscripts. The Grolier Codex, which was written around 1230 A.D., and the Dresden Codex, written just before the Spanish conquest, have tables for the plotting of the phases of Venus, Mars, and solar eclipses.

Maya Writing

One of the great achievements of the Maya civilization was the development of a system of writing. The decipherment of the Maya codices, relief carvings on buildings, and the memorial stelae (primarily erected in cities of the southern lowlands) was a challenge to archaeologists until it was discovered that the writing system consisted of a combination of glyphs or signs and phonetic symbols that could be used in combination to spell out a name. For instance the word jaguar or *balam* could be represented by the head of a jaguar or it could be indicated by a jaguar head combined with phonetic signs that spelled *ba*, *la* and *ma*. Phonetic signs also were used independent of the glyph. Mayan was written in two columns and was read in rows from left to right over the columns.

The Ball Game

Mayan Ball Court

In most Maya cities that have been excavated, there is at least one ball court, indicating the central importance of the game now referred to as pok-ta-pok. The long rectangular structures with sloping or vertical walls along the sides were the sites of a game in which two teams of 2-7 people moved a rubber ball by hitting it with the body without the use of hands or feet. The most effective method of directing the ball was through the use of the hips. The goal was to pass the ball through a vertical circular ring attached to the long wall of the court. This game or a variant of it was important in several Mesoamerican cultures, but based on the archeological evidence the Maya considered it to be a central feature in their urban life. Sculpture associated with ball courts suggest that the game concluded with ritual human sacrifice, presumably captives, although some have suggested that the losing team or the captain of the team were treated to sacrificial execution. This procedure makes sense in the light of the theory that the game was a way of settling municipal grievances or inter-city wars. If the game was merely played for the sake of entertainment and competition, a ritual sacrifice of the losers would have been a rather severe method of improving the quality of play.

Chapter 6: Cities of the Maya

The Maya had a unique urban culture that is evident from both the remains of their earliest settlements in the highlands of Guatemala and the last of the great Maya cities, Mayapán in the Yucatan. The planning of Maya cities, the arrangement of buildings in the center, and the disposition of small farms and dwellings forming the urban area remained generally consistent throughout the centuries, regardless of the different developments of their culture.

The first great Maya city that has been discovered is the recently excavated El Mirador in Guatemala. Archaeologists believe that it flourished between 200 B.C.-150 A.D. and had a population in the tens of thousands spread over nearly 10 square miles. As was common among the Maya, part of the city of El Mirador is built on the foundations of prior construction dating from the Middle Preclassic Period. The central east-west axis of the city joins two massive complexes separated by over a mile. At one end the tallest Maya pyramid rising over 200 feet dominates a plaza and two lateral temples. On the lower levels of these temples, archaeologists unearthed stucco jaguar masks, and adjacent to these temples is a burial acropolis which held the bodies of priests and noblemen surrounded by obsidian lancets and stingray spines. These tools were used to pierce the penis, ears and tongue in bloodletting rituals that were common in all great Maya cities. Bloodletting was a means to invoke the gods and ensure their presence in the Mayans' lives. On the other end of the city axis at El Mirador, a slightly lower pyramid is flanked by two temples. The size and complexity of the city of El Mirador makes clear that even during the so-called Preclassic Era, the Maya civilization had reached a particularly high level of architectural, artistic and social sophistication.

The Temple at Tikal

The city of Tikal, also in the Guatemalan highland rainforest, is an example of a Classic Maya city. At the site of Tikal a modest village was established perhaps as early as 900 B.C., and as archaeological evidence suggests, some 400 years later the population had expanded to a level sufficient for the construction of a small astronomical temple. After 250 B.C., the first ceremonial buildings were erected, including a pyramid and modest temples. The Great Plaza of Tikal begun around the beginning of the Common Era was followed by massive construction that stretched over the next 200 years. This increasingly elaborate architecture and decoration formed the basis for re-building and expansion of the ceremonial precincts in the classic period from 400 to 909 CE when Tikal reached the zenith of its power even though it suffered from unsuccessful wars with Caracol in modern Belize. A great deal is known about the dynastic history of Tikal and its various wars and alliances with neighbouring cities. One King Hasaw Chan K'awil waged a successful campaign in 696 against the city of Calakmul which had at one point overrun Tikal. In a period of peace Hasaw Chan K'awil's son Yik'in Chan K'awil launched a building campaign creating five of Tikal's most important temples. In one of them he entombed his father's body. Around the year 900 Tikal collapsed and was abandoned.

Uxmal

In the Late Classic Period, from 600-950 A.D., the Maya cities of the Yucatan flourished. The best known of these are a cluster of sites in the Puuc hills south of the modern city of Mérida. The most elaborate and finest of Maya architecture is found here cities like Uxmal, Sayil and Kabah. At Uxmal, the *ahau* or king, known as Lord Chak (c. 890-910), was responsible for the construction of several of the major structures, including what is known as the Nunnery and the Governor's Palace. The decoration of these building with intricate relief carvings on inset flat and bowed stones, and the use of three dimensional mosaic patterns in the masonry, represents the zenith of the Mayans' architectural finesse.

The cities of the Puuc hills seem to have had a peaceful cooperative relationship with each other. Roads with cut stone curbs connected them together, and one of the roads that ran from Kabah to Uxmal was decorated with the largest extant Maya monumental corbelled arch. The Maya did not have in their repertoire of architectural forms an arch with a keystone, rather they used the corbelled arch in which from the springing of the arch stones in successive courses are offset. The corbelled arch required massive amounts of masonry to ensure stability and had a limited span, so arched interior rooms in Maya temples and other structures are long and narrow.

Arch over the road from Kabah to Uxmal, Kabah (Photo: Alan McNairn)

The most visited and the most spectacular of Late Classic Maya cities is Chichén Itzá, which was very large and became a very influential center in the later years of Maya civilization. With a spectacular pyramid, enormous ball court, observatory and several temples, the builders of this city exceeded even those at Uxmal in developing the use of columns and exterior relief decoration. Of particular interest at Chichén Itzá is the sacred cenote, which is accessed by a road from the central plaza. The cenote or sinkhole was a focus for Maya rituals around water. Because adequate supplies of water, which rarely collected on the surface of the limestone based Yucatan, were essential for adequate agricultural production, the Maya here considered it of primary importance. Underwater archaeology carried out in the cenote at Chichén Itzá revealed that offerings to the Maya rain deity Chaac (which may have included people) were tossed into the sinkhole. Chichén Itzá had a relatively short period of dominance in the region, lasting from about 800-950 A.D.

Ruins at Chichén Itzá

El Castillo or Pyramid, Chichén Itzá

The last city of the Maya to rise to prominence was Mayapán in the Yucatan. Its glory days were around 1200 CE, and it collapsed just before the arrival of the Spanish. The finish and decoration of the buildings in this city are considered to be significantly less accomplished than those in the earlier Maya communities, because the builders apparently used less than exacting standards. This approach to the archaeological evidence of Mayapán is based on the long accepted chronology of Maya civilization which placed emphasis on art and architectural achievements of the Classic Period, a designation based on the quality of the elite material culture. Archaeology was at one point an essential supplier of museum exhibits, and up until very recently, museums had very little interest in displaying the mundane everyday objects of a culture. Still, it is important to remember that the supposed decline of architecture and architectural ornament at Mayapán should not be taken as an indicator of the decline of Maya civilization. After all, today's modern cities often involve varying degrees of quality, even in the same city. Certain areas of Queens do not resemble the Upper West Side of Manhattan, but that hardly means New York City is in decline.

Chapter 7: The Collapse and Resurrection of Maya Culture

Eventually the great Maya cities began to lose their populations, one by one. The collapse came first to the cities of the southern lowlands. For example, building came to a halt and ritual ceremonies were abandoned at Palenque in 799 and Tikal in 879. In the northern lowlands of the

Yucatan, the cities of the Puuc hills such as Uxmal were abandoned starting around 920, and Chichén Itzá was partially abandoned in 948. The culture of the Maya survived in a disorganized way until it was revived at Mayapán around 1200.

Why Maya cities were abandoned and left to be overgrown by the jungle is a puzzle that intrigues curious people around the world today, especially those who have a penchant for speculating on lost civilizations. Often, conjecture on the cause of the end of the Maya civilization has depended on the preconceptions of the observer. If one were to ask Bishop Landa why the Maya he met and talked to were in such a sorry state he would have said that their condition was a result of their unbaptized state. Some American archaeologists, living in the era of frighteningly bloody mass wars of the 20th century, suggested that the Maya destroyed themselves by constant inter-city warfare. Others writing in the era of the rise of Communism believed that Maya cities collapsed because of class warfare. In the 21st century, a more common theory on the collapse of the Maya is that they were forced by drought, overpopulation and unsustainable agricultural practices to move away from their urban centres. What probably happened was that some or all these social and environmental factors (with the exception of Landa's religious notions) converged in such a way that even the strongest of Maya cities were unable to survive.

As it was, the Maya civilization was already in a serious state of decline when the Europeans arrived in their territory. The Spanish did their best to ensure that the final nail was driven into the Maya coffin, both through the spread of warfare and disease, but the Mayan culture was never completely eradicated.

The Caste War

In the struggle for independence in Mexico, the elite of the Yucatan opted for a federalist model of administration for the new country. In 1838 Yucatecos revolted against the interference of the government in Mexico City and in the years following engaged in armed struggle to defend the virtual independence of the Yucatan. In this struggle they enlisted Maya as cannon fodder and promised them remission of taxes and monies paid to the church. The Yucatec authorities did not honor their agreement and in 1847 Maya troops revolted in Valladolid. Using the weapons that they retained from service in the Yucatec army and weapons supplied by the British through Belize, the Maya insurgents in the Caste War, as it came to be known, almost succeeded taking over the entire Yucatan. On the eve of what would have been a successful siege of Mérida, the Maya soldiers gave up and returned to their fields. Pursued by the Yucatec forces the Maya melted into the jungle and formed communities that exist to this day.

Modern Maya Culture

If one accepts the premise that language is the core of culture, then the Maya culture is alive and well in Mexico and Central America. Some 6 million people in the region speak in one of the Mayan group of languages, and many still adhere to a system of beliefs that combines ancient Mayan religion and Catholicism. Moreover, there is a rich tradition of post-colonial literature in the Mayan language written in Latin script.

   Given the world's strong and ongoing interest in the Maya, it seems certain that the culture and legacy of the Maya will never go extinct.

The Aztec

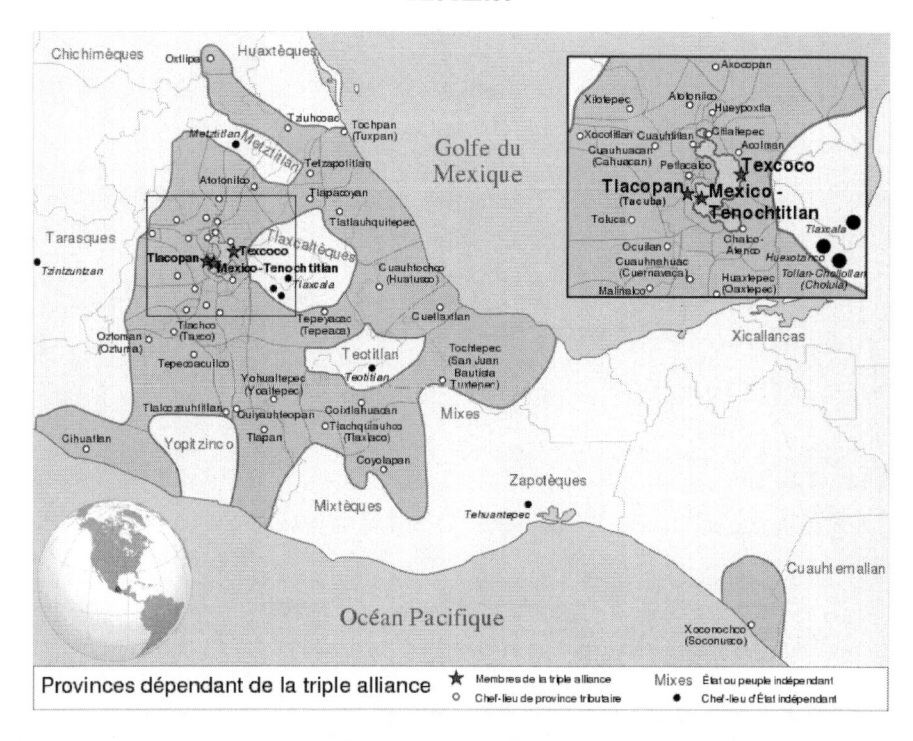

Map of the Aztec Empire

Chapter 1: The History of the Aztecs

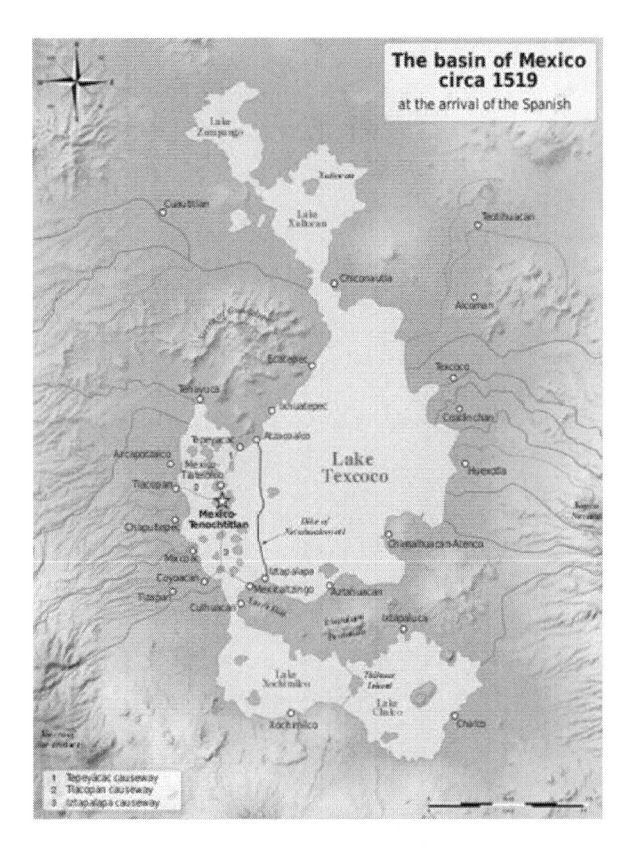

When the origins of the Aztecs were historically revised by Montezuma I during the middle of the 15th century, it obscured the fact that the Aztecs were relative newcomers to the lands that eventually formed their vast empire. The Aztecs, or Mexica as they called themselves, arrived in the valley of Mexico in the mid-13th century. These Nahuatl speaking people, according to their own recorded history, came from an apparently mythical city named Aztlan to the north. Aztlan was located on a beautiful island in a lake, which was convenient since Tenochtitlan was built on an island in Lake Texcoco. Given that the Aztecs were adept at rewriting their history to suit current needs, the story of Aztlan may very well have been concocted long after their settlement in the Valley of Mexico. It is likely that the Aztec people came from somewhere in the modern state of Nayarit in Mexico, which is on the country's west coast, touching the Pacific Ocean.

There were other Nahuatl speaking people in the Valley of Mexico when the Aztecs arrived, so, despite their travels, they were not actually a distinct tribe or race. Instead, they distinguished themselves by forging a cultural, political and ideological identity, accomplished in party by adopting and adapting various aspects of the diverse cultures and religions of central Mexico that came over a millennium before them. In fact, when the Aztecs built their major cities, they were similar in many respects to Teotihuacan, built by a still unidentified people around 100 B.C.–250 A.D. The Aztecs adopted as their central divinity Huizilopochtli, a classic Toltec god, and transformed the theocracy surrounding his worship of 4 priest rulers into a single monarchy.

Although they would come to be known as one of the greatest conquering civilizations in the hemisphere, the Aztecs seemingly lost one of their first important battles. The Aztecs first attempted to settle in Chapultepec on the shore of Lake Texcoco but were expelled from the city. They then moved further south to Culhuacán, a late Toltec state, where they served as mercenaries. This alliance ended in rather gruesome circumstances. It is said that the Aztecs asked the ruler of Culhuacán for a bride for their ruler. A princess was provided, but instead of forming a marital alliance the Aztecs killed her and then flayed her. When a priest appeared wearing her skin, the people of Culhuacán, justifiably horrified, expelled the Aztecs from their territory.

Founding of Tenochtitlan, from the Codex Mendoza, circa 1541. Bodleian Library Oxford

In 1325, the wandering Aztecs came upon an island in Lake Texcoco where, according to their history, they saw an eagle roosting on a cactus devouring a nopal or prickly pear. They identified the eagle as Huizilopochtli, their war and hunting deity, and the red fruit of the nopal as a heart. The island, again according to the Aztec history that was rewritten at the height of their power, was a twin to their original home of Atzlan.

For much of the 14th century, while they built their city of Tenochtitlan, the Aztecs were vassals to the more powerful cities around the lake. While building their great city, they divided it into four quarters, and the quarters were divided into calpulli or, in more modern terms, wards. These city districts, 24 in all, were made up of families that were connected through kinship, and the calpulli had community temples, markets, schools and administrative offices. The calpulli were led by elders who may have been hereditary office holders, and these elders represented their calpulli and formed the governing body of the city of Tenochtitlan. They even appointed the king and exercised control over the management of the growing metropolis.

If that arrangement doesn't sound right, that's because over time the control exercised by the calpulli and their elders over the king diminished. Instead, the administration and control of the royal household became the prerogative of a priestly and warrior elite, and the undemocratic turn of events often meant that control of the Aztec city required coercion to ensure the loyalty of the people of the calpulli.

From 1409-1428, there was a substantial realignment of power in the Valley of Mexico. The Aztecs negotiated an alliance or confederation between the cities of Tenochtitlan and its immediate neighbor on Lake Taxcoco, Tlacopan and the city of Texcoco on the east side of the lake. Commonly referred to as the Triple Alliance, it allowed the Aztecs to engage in expansion without the constant threat of aggression from their powerful neighbors.

In 1426, the royal palace elite of Tenochtitlan elevated the war lord Itzacóatl (native for obsidian serpent) to the throne, and he chose as his second in command, Cihuacoatl (snake woman). Together they set about consolidating their empire by subduing the cities around the lake, which were then required to render tribute to the Aztec king. He was succeeded by Moctezuma I (or Montezuma I, who ruled from 1440-1468. Along with his younger brother Tlacaélel, they expanded the Aztec tributary region, and the Aztec empire was further consolidated and expanded by Ahuitzotl, who assumed power in 1486. The final and most famous ruler was Moctequma II (often referred to as Montezuma II or simply Montezuma by those unaware of the first leader of the same name decades earlier), who reigned from 1503 until his murder in the presence of the conquistadors during a riot in 1520.

Under this set of kings the notion of equality in Tenochtitlan was further eroded. The rise of absolute imperial power also coincided with the increasing importance place in the imperial cult of Huitzilopochli, who was rewarded with increasing attention in rituals of sacrifice.

Chapter 2: The Aztec Empire

The rise of the absolutely powerful Aztec ruler was made possible by a compact with the people of Tenochtitlan in 1420. In exchange for military victory and all it implied in terms of greater municipal stability, increased quantities of tribute, food and prosperity, the political power of the calpulli and the community elders was forfeited.

The territory over which the Aztecs held control expanded quickly under the rule of the all powerful kings. This was the period of what has been called the Aztec Empire, though calling it an empire is somewhat a misnomer. Unlike other historical empires, the Aztecs did not actually occupy or govern the people they conquered within their empire. When they conquered a city, the Aztecs acquired captives and the right to tribute, which was to be sent to Tenochtitlan according to a regular schedule. Since the Aztecs did not leave behind administrators or a garrison but merely went home with their captives, it was left up to the conquered city to render tribute when it was due. Those cities that reneged would be subject to a renewed attack in which more captives were taken and more tribute was demanded. Making this arrangement even more unique, the Aztecs did not maintain a standing army; their empire was controlled or policed by warriors assembled on an ad hoc basis. That they proved so successful and conquered such a large area is all the more remarkable.

The Aztecs' expansion was out of necessity. When Tenochtitlan suffered food shortages caused by increased population and/or crop failures, their warriors were dispatched to subjugate new territories and win more tribute. Of course, as time went on the new tribute cities were located further and further away from the capital, and the Aztecs found the land to the west and north was not productive enough to warrant imperial expansion. To the south, the tribute cities provided luxury goods but were too far distant to provide a source for food. So it was to the east that the Aztecs began expanding their empire. But the increasing distances of the tribute cities made the food distribution system less and less efficient as the empire expanded, because the Aztecs lacked wheeled vehicles and customary beasts of burden.

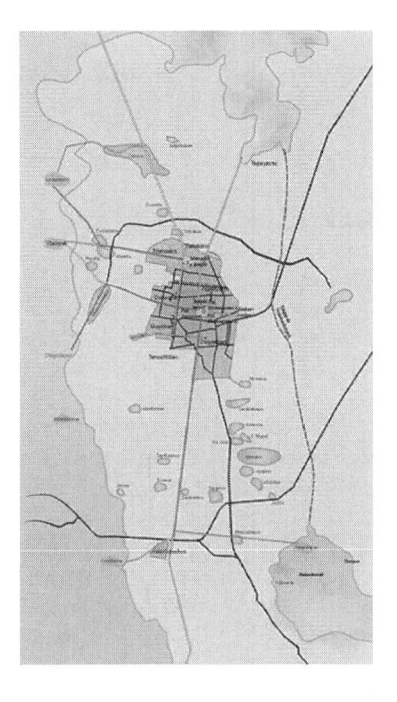

Tenochtitland and the islands in Lake Texcoco. Map by Hanns Penn

As a result, the Aztecs had to rely on human porters to transport the incoming tribute, which posed a unique problem of its own. The further these human porters had to carry food, the more of it they consumed along the way. Thus, the most important cities within the empire that supplied food to the Aztecs were within easy reach of Lake Taxcoco.

Another important aspect of the transportation system was the fact that the Aztecs' capital was literally on an island, which required using water for travel and transportation. Plying the waters of lagoons or lakes in the Valley of Mexico, there were as many as 10,000 canoes, some as long as 50 feet. These vessels brought goods across Lake Texcoco from lakeshore farms and villages, as well as tribute carried from more distant vassal towns.

The farms in the lagoons of the Valley of Mexico were peculiar to the environment. Building in the region was accomplished using an agricultural technique, by building up mounds of earth in the shallow waters. In essence, the natives were able to create floating islands by excavating the mud from the lake's bottom and piling it up on beds of reeds, a feat that astounded the Europeans that first bore witness to them. Some of these chinampas were nearly 100 feet long. These unique farms were particularly productive, but they were naturally vulnerable to the changes in water level. Chinampas are still in cultivation at Xochimilco, now an ecological preserve in Mexico City. The Aztec chinampas farming eventually covered some 25,000 acres or 10,000 hectares in the lagoons around Lake Taxcoco.

King Ahuítzotl (1486-1501) was especially successful in expanding the economic empire to include the cities of Mitla and Oxaca, and parts of present day Guatemala and El Salvador. From this region, the Aztecs demanded tribute in the form of cotton, jade, jewels, feathers and cocoa. In 1440, the city of Taxco was subjugated, from which was sent cotton, honey, and copal to Tenochtitlan as tribute. In the far reaches of the southern part of their empire, the Aztecs installed pochteca or merchants who, in the absence of any currency among the Aztecs, probably were agents of trade exchanging manufactured luxury goods for the raw materials required by the artisans of Tenochtitlan for their manufacture.

Given this system, the Aztec Empire was essentially an agrarian one. The tribute delivered to Tenochtitlan was the property of the elites, who also received an "in kind" tax from the common farmers and fishermen of the city. They distributed the surplus in the form of gifts to the populace to keep everyone happy. Thus, the economy of the Aztec Empire has been described as redistributive in the form of a highly organized potlatch state.

Chapter 3: The Aztec City of Tenochtitlan

Today Tenochtitlan is mostly remembered for being a floating island city, made all the more ironic by the fact that it was essentially the forerunner of Mexico City, one of the biggest cities in the world today. Lake Texcoco was part of a closed river basin consisting of shallow lakes, lagoons and marshes that formed during the period of glaciation and received additional waters during the annual rainy season. It was on this lake that the floating city was created.

Because the existence of Tenochtitlan depended on water management for the safety of the city, the Aztecs developed ingenious waterworks to facilitate agriculture and the movement of goods. Aqueducts supplied the drinking water, while canals, wharves and flood control gates enabled reliable waterborne commerce. The Aztecs maintained control of the input of water into the lakes and marshes, keeping the salt content of the otherwise closed system under control. Though they accomplished this with hard labor, the Aztecs ensured that Tláloc, the god of water who controlled rain and storms, was content, with one of the two elevated sanctuaries on the great central pyramid of Tenochtitlan was dedicated to Tláloc.

Tlaloc, Codex Rios, after 1566. Vatican Library

Fresh water was first supplied to the city by means of two channels made of reeds and mud that ran from Chapultepec, and reservoirs were constructed in Tenochtitlan from which residents obtained their water for household use. The two channels also delivered water to underground aqueducts that supplied the palaces of the elite in the center of the city. The running water was used to supply the many baths in the palaces, as well as pools and irrigated gardens.

At the height of the Aztec empire, a more ambitious aqueduct was constructed between Chapultepec and the city, spanning nearly 10 miles. This aqueduct was over 20 feet wide. As the city grew further and more water was required, another elaborate aqueduct was constructed in 1499 to bring water from five springs that fed into a dammed basin in Coyoacán. Lacking a control mechanism to prevent exceptional water flow from coursing down the spill way into the city, the aqueduct actually proved to be a hazard to the inhabitants of Tenochtitlan. In 1500, when there were unprecedented rains, the city suffered a disastrous flood partly due to the rising water level in Lake Texcoco but more importantly from this unstoppable aqueduct.

The Aztecs used a considerable amount of water for bathing and washing their streets, with thousands of laborers watering and sweeping the streets daily. The elite classes also kept themselves clean by using soap to bathe, and according to the Spanish, Montezuma bathed twice a day in tubs in the royal palace. He apparently changed his clothes frequently as well.

The Aztecs were meticulous in the control of waste. No solid waste was disposed of through the drainage pipes that emptied into the lake. Care was taken to collect solid waste and what was appropriate was taken to the chiampas for use as fertilizer.

By the time Tenochtitlan was taken by the Spanish, it spanned some 1,000 hectares, the equivalent of 10 million square meters. The incredible size and organization of Tenochtitlan was so impressive to the conquistadors that some of them compared it to Venice. The population size also astonished the conquistadors, who found one well organized market in which 60,000 people were carrying on business. The market had a huge variety of goods for exchange, and nearby were a number of studios where highly skilled artisans worked and sold their goods.

Model of Temple Precinct at Tenochtitlan. Photo: Thelmadatter

The city centered on the walled square of the Great Temple and adjacent residences of the king, priests and elite warriors. The streets were laid out in a grid pattern interspersed by canals in each of the quarters and their constituent calpulli or wards. Causeways connected the city to the mainland, alongside which ran the aqueducts.

Ruins of Templo Mayor

In the center of Tenochtitlan was a walled precinct. The wall was decorated on the outside with snakes, earning it the name *coatepantli* or serpent wall. It contained a large square, the enormous pyramidal Templo Mayor. The Templo Mayor or Great Temple was rebuilt several times over, with the new and improved structure simply constructed over the previous and less elevated pyramid. The last version of the Templo Mayor was dedicated in 1487 and reached a height of about 130 feet.

Model of the Temple

The pyramid was capped by two temples, with one dedicated to Huizilopochtli and the other to Tláloc. The idea of capping a pyramid with twin temples was derived from earlier post classic construction at such sites as Tula and Teotihuacán. Though the Mayans are the ones remembered for their mastery of astronomy, the Aztecs' temples were oriented in such a way as to emphasize the seasonal movement of the sun. In the wetter season, the sun rose behind the Temple of Tláloc, and in the summer it rose behind the Temple of Huizilopochtli. On the two equinoctial days the sun rose between the two temples and shone on the Temple of Quetzalcoatl that faced the Templo Mayor.

In the walled central temple enclosure there were five other structures. Among them were the Temple of Xipe Totec and the Temple of Tezcatlipoca. Included in the central temple enclosure was also a ball court where it is presumed religiously based athletic competitions were held. The exact nature of the Aztec ball game is unknown, but it is likely that it was similar to that in other Mesoamerican cities and involved teams hitting a ball through a goal using their hips or chests or heads.

The common people of Tenochtitlan lived in houses that fronted on the streets of their calpulli. The adobe or wattle and daub houses were L-shaped, enclosing an interior courtyard in which most of the domestic activities were carried out. Here the women spun thread and wove fabric, ground corn, baked tortillas, prepared food and interacted with kin who came and went with little formality. The domestic court was the site of family festivals celebrating the birth or naming of a child, in which quantities of food were given to friends, neighbors and the hungry poor. The common men worked on their chinampas or fished in the lake.

Estimates of the population of Tenochtitlan vary considerably, but it is likely that the total population of the city was in the range of 200,000 to 300,000 most of which would have been of the common class. It is probable that the second largest segment of the population were slaves. The sheer number of people in Tenochtitlan amazed the conquistadors, who compared the size of the city to some of the largest municipalities at home in Spain. Incredibly, the city had amenities that were unthought of even in Europe. For example, there were schools for children of all classes, even commoners. Adjacent to the local temple the schools provided instruction for children from 7 to 14 years in age with boys and girls taught in separate rooms. Children were taught the history of the Aztecs, dancing, singing, public speaking and were even given religious instruction. The schools for children of the elite were located in the center of Tenochtitlan. There they were taught a broader curriculum that included astronomy, arithmetic, oratory, reading and writing.

The priestly and elite warrior class dwelt in more luxurious palaces located near the royal palace around the central temple precinct. These buildings were presumably highly decorated with relief sculptures and may have been colorfully painted outside and inside.

The king lived on the second floor of his palace with two wives and 150 concubines as well as a great number of servants, guards and attendants. To feed this vast crowd the palace had extensive kitchens and store rooms. Celebratory banquets included a variety of tempting dishes, including frogs with green peppers, sage locusts and nopal with fish eggs. As many as 300 guests were fed at special banquets. While the king ate with his guests, he was hidden behind a screen during the meal.

The highly stratified society of the Aztecs involved the regulation of various rights and privileges of the inhabitants of Tenochtitlan. For example, Montezuma I enacted a series of precise sumptuary laws prohibiting commoners from wearing cotton or a cloak falling below the knee. Commoners were also forbidden to wear sandals in the city streets, while specific kinds of cloaks, jewels and decoration were prescribed as appropriate to various levels of society and different ranks of warriors.

Chapter 4: The Aztec Religion and Human Sacrifice Rituals

Aztec Ritual Sacrifice, Codex Tudela, 16th century based on an earlier work. Museo de América, Madrid

More is known about Aztec religious practices than any other aspect of their culture, mostly because the major element in the public ceremonies was focused on human sacrifice. The rituals were apparently so gruesome that they horrified even the Spanish, who were not exactly known for their gentility when it came to war and religious fervor.

Although some have suggested other theories to explain the large amount of human sacrifices, including political intimidation and even as a means of population control, it is still widely believed that it had religious symbolism. Thus, the Aztecs, either to please the gods or ensure their constant attention to earthly life, frequently bestowed on them the gift of sacrificial humans. This in itself was not unique to the region, as it was a well documented practice among other Mesoamerican civilizations. In fact, the Aztecs' enemy, the Tlaxcala, sacrificed captured Aztecs, and some of their accounts suggest it was considered an honor to die as a sacrifice. And human sacrifice in and of itself would not have been particularly upsetting to the Spanish, nor would it have been of great interest to generations of readers on the Aztecs.

However, the brutality, quantity and method of disposal of human remains as practiced by the Aztecs almost defy the imagination. An example of the rite of human sacrifice at its height was that performed for the dedication of the new Templo Mayor in 1487. The ceremony lasted four days, during which anywhere from 4,000 to 20,000 humans were sacrificed. As proof of their zeal, Aztec accounts themselves placed the number over 80,000, which would have required sacrificing over a dozen people a minute. Captives from the Huastec region to the east of Tenochtitlan were paraded through the temple square joined by ropes threaded through their pierced noses. They climbed one by one up the steep steps of the pyramid to the temples at the top where they were laid over a stone. A priest wielding an obsidian-bladed ritual knife hacked open the victim's chest, tore out the still beating heart and placed it in a basin where it was incinerated. The body of the victim was kicked off the temple platform and rolled down to the square below. Here it was dismembered. The skull was installed on a rack and the limbs were distributed to the crowd assembled in the square.

A tzompantli or skull rack, Ramirez Codex, late 16th century. Museum of Anthropology, Mexico City

Temple Sacrifice. Codex Magliabechiano, mid 16th century based on an earlier codex. Biblioteca Nazionale Centrale, Florence

The ceremonial dedication of the Templo Mayor may have been on a grander scale than day to day ritual sacrifice, but the number of victims of Aztec religious practices was always high.

When Cortés' men were shown into the temples of Tenochtitlan in 1519, they were nauseated by the stench of the burning hearts and the blood soaked walls. Bernal Diaz described what he saw in one of the temples. On these altars were idols, with evil looking bodies, he reported, and every night five captives were sacrificed before them. Their chests were cut open, and their arms and thighs were cut off. The walls of the temple were covered with blood. "We stood greatly amazed and gave the island the name *isleta de Sacrificios* (Island of the Sacrifices)."

Describing one sacrifice in detail, he wrote:

"They strike open the wretched Indian's chest with flint knives and hastily tear out the palpitating heart which, with the blood, they present to the idols […]. They cut off the arms, thighs and head, eating the arms and thighs at ceremonial banquets. The head they hang up on a beam, and the body is […] given to the beasts of prey."

The beasts of prey were the animals in Montequma's zoo. Diaz continues:

"They have a most horrid and abominable custom which truly ought to be punished and which until now we have seen in no other part, and this is that, whenever they wish to ask something of the idols, in order that their plea may find more acceptance, they take many girls and boys and even adults, and in the presence of these idols they open their chests while they are still alive and take out their hearts and entrails and burn them before the idols, offering the smoke as sacrifice. Some of us have seen this, and they say it is the most terrible and frightful thing they have ever witnessed."

Victim of Sacrificial Gladitorial Combat Holding a Feather Club, Codex Magliabechiano, mid 16th century. Biblioteca Nazionale Centrale, Florence

The disposal of the remains from the temple rites has been the subject of heated debate among academics who study the Aztecs. What is indisputable is the fact that they were carried to the homes around the city and cooked up and eaten, leaving scholars to perform all kinds of academic gymnastics attempting to explain Aztec cannibalism. Current studies suggest that the Aztecs were cannibals because this was the only reliable source of protein in their diets. Completely lacking domesticated animals, with the exception of birds, and suffering from periodic food shortages, the Aztecs for their very survival required a constant supply of human flesh. This came not only from the temples in the central complex but also from neighborhood temples in the calpulli.

Whatever the case, the supply of sacrificial victims was clearly a constant concern for the Aztecs. It is possible that one of the reasons the Aztecs did not have a standing army and did not install garrisons in the conquered towns around the empire was that they needed the people who would've occupied those cities to capture and bring back as many captives as possible for sacrifice. There must have been a constant coming and going of warriors who marched off to the cities and towns in the empire and captured as many prisoners as were required. This periodic harvesting of victims required that outlying cities not be pacified nor included within an organized Aztec administration.

Aztec warriors, literally fighting for dinner, sometimes engaged in battles with the consent of the opposition. In these cases, it seems the conflicts were a form of recreation. If they were not fought for entertainment, then battle was a way for warriors of both sides to enhance their status.

The Aztecs called their expeditions to gather sacrificial victim flower or flowery wars because the captives were rounded up and carried home like a garland of blooms. In the 1400s the Aztecs conducted many campaigns of flowery wars. Tlacaélel, brother of Moctezuma I and his chief military advisor or cihuacóatl, is reported to have said these expeditions were like buying food in a market. He was of the opinion that, when faced with the need for victims to serve in the inauguration of the Great Temple, the god Huitzilopochtli did not need to wait for a quarrel to instigate a war. For the market, said Tlacaélel, the Aztecs did not need travel to the far realms; instead they could capture their victims from cities close at hand. This required that the battles should not be decisive so that Huitzilopochtli could feed at pleasure just like man enjoying a freshly baked tortilla.

When the Aztec army was on a "hunting" expedition, they marched in a long ordered procession behind scouts. The first combatants were the warrior priests, who carried a banner or images of Huitzilopochtli. Following them were the warrior elite, including the tlatoani (commander in chief) or king. Trailing this group were the ordinary warriors. In battle, the Aztecs fought with short javelins and clubs fitted with obsidian blades. Since captives for sacrifice were the objective, the best warriors did not kill or seriously maim their opponents.

The victims taken to Tenochtitlan were well taken care of before suffering their fate. Warriors might claim a special victim that they had personally captured, and that captive would be well fed and tended in a cage. When he was dispatched by the priest, his limbs would be given to the warrior who had captured him. The warrior, who would have been among the 400 men put forth by each calpulli and who fought under a ward banner, celebrated his skill by inviting a number of people to join him in partaking of the special meal. The poor might also crowd into the party in the hopes that some scraps would be given to them.

The execution of captives varied depending on the god to which they were sacrificed. For example, in the temple dedicated to Mixocoatl, the god of hunting, a victim was shot full of arrows before his heart was removed and he was dismembered.

The festival of Tlacaxipehualiztli (flaying of men), celebrated annually just before the rainy season, was held at the temple of Xipe Totec, "our lord the flayed one", the sun god. The victims who had been well treated, perhaps even revered prior to the festival, were dressed in costumes to appear like Xipe Totec. They were tied to large stones and armed with feather encrusted weapons to fight off the advances of five warriors who were armed with spears and obsidian bladed clubs. The blood of the victims fed the earth and ensured a good planting season. The victims' bodies were flayed, and the priests of the temple wore their skins for 20 days.

Chapter 5: Aztec Art and Architecture

Describing the Aztec civilization as paradoxical is an understatement. Indeed, given today's preoccupation with their ritual sacrifice, "Aztec civilization" seems an oxymoron. It is almost impossible to understand how the same people who were meticulous with regard to cleanliness and who created magnificent architectural monuments and decorative art could also be cannibals whose religion centered on violently bloody and stench inducing practices.

Nevertheless, the Aztecs demonstrated remarkable skill in their creation of art, both in depictions of some of the more savage aspects of their culture and others. Disregarding the subject of some of the pieces of Aztec art, their surviving art indicates a remarkable sensitivity to form and composition, and they reveal unusually accomplished techniques of execution.

Unfortunately, much of their art was destroyed. After the conquest of the Aztecs by Cortés, the city of Tenochtitlan was leveled, and those Aztecs who escaped the Spaniards' swords and the new European diseases dispersed in the region. Some were artisans who continued to produce work in the Aztec style. Meanwhile, the buildings of Tenochtitlan were mined for materials to construct a new city on the site so that until recently there were no tangible remains of the buildings of the once mighty Aztecs. Because of the nature of their empire, the Aztec culture did not penetrate into the cities that provided tribute. Still, there was some export of the exquisite decorative art of the Aztecs, and bits and pieces have been found around the vassal states.

Coatlicue, Museum of Anthropology, Mexico City Photo: Rosemania

For the most part, the treasures that Cortés and his followers extracted from Tenochtitlan itself were melted down or otherwise destroyed. The first shipment of the fifth part of the treasure that was owed to the king of Spain arrived in Brussels in 1520. It was inspected by the German graphic artist Albrecht Dürer, who was quite familiar with precious metals because his father was a goldsmith. He was very impressed by a gold sun and a silver moon that he said were nearly two meters in size. The shipment, which also included exotic costumes, weapons and metalwork was, according to Durer, extremely valuable. He wrote, "I have seen amongst them wonderfully artistic things, and have wondered at the subtle *Ingenia* of men in foreign lands."

What little that remained of Aztec art at Tenochtitlan was destroyed by zealous priests who quickly appeared to convert the survivors of Cortés' program of pacification. Aztec manuscripts were incinerated, but a few survived, and these were copied by later descendants of the Aztecs. The decorative sculpture that adorned the palaces and temples of Tenochtitlan were destroyed or remains buried beneath Mexico City. Thus, building material for the new Templo Mayor, the Cathedral of Mexico City, was readily at hand in the levelled Aztec temple precinct.

Perhaps not surprisingly, given its central role in their lives, Aztec sculpture is rife with the theme of blood sacrifice. To the Spanish these pagan idols were almost as horrifying as the practices they referred to. One of Cortés' soldiers recorded that when he saw these gold and jewel encrusted images in a temple in Tenochtitlan, they were covered in blood.

A sculpture of Coatlicue, or "she of the serpent skirt", found in the temple precinct in the 18th century, is a truly frightening image. The severed head is replaced by two facing serpent heads, and another snake moves down from the groin. The hands and feet of the god are clawed, and she has a necklace decorated with severed hands and hearts. In Aztec mythology, Coatlicue was the mother of Huitzilopochtli, who was delivered from her after she had been decapitated by her enemies. Coatlicue lived in a temple on a rise called the hill of snakes.

The sculpture of Coatlicue, reflecting in its double snake head the twin temples atop the Great Pyramid at Tenochtitlan, is illustrative of Aztec craftsmanship and concepts of pictorial representation. The entire surface is taken up with complex decoration so that the image is an intricate pattern. Great care was taken in the incision of lines, combined with smoothly rounded forms. While it is hard to imagine today, the impact of this image would have been even more extraordinary than it already is, because it was originally painted in bright colors and peppered with applied jewels and gold.

The Great Calendar Stone, Museum of Anthropology, Mexico City. Photo: Rosemania

Also found near the Cathedral in Mexico City in the 18th century was what is popularly known as the Great Calendar Stone. It is possibly the most famous piece of Aztec art, having been reproduced a countless number of times to provide tourist souvenirs. In this brilliant work, the intricate precision of Aztec sculptors is clear. In the center is the face of a female earth monster, framed by clawed arms that hold human hearts. This is encircled by signs of the four suns, representing destructions of the world. The next circle has representations of the names of the 20 days in the Aztec calendar. When the contents of the entire disk are considered, it is clear that this is a symbolic representation of the end of the world. This stone was probably not part of the architectural decoration of a temple; it was probably laid out flat and served as a site of sacrifice to prevent the end of the world.

Pendant Mask, at the Louvre, Paris

Aztec artisans produced three dimensional sculptures that were often quite distinct from the highly patterned relief style. A highly polished jade pendant mask, probably representing Xipe Totec, is a remarkably powerful image. The bilaterally symmetrical face has a charm that people today probably would not associate with the Aztecs, but this is probably due to our own aesthetic predispositions. There is no doubt that the sculptor intended this image to be a sign of the ferocious nature of the god.

Eagle Warrior. Museum of Anthropology, Mexico City. Photo: Maunus

A four piece life-sized ceramic sculpture of an eagle warrior also indicates the Aztec ability to create simple forms that are quite unlike the reliefs described above. This piece is evidence of the remarkable technical ability of the Aztecs to make large ceramic works. The naturalistic hands and feet, and the smoothly rounded forms of the body and face, again appeal to our modern eyes. What we appreciate in the simplicity and clarity of the warrior was probably not so clear in its original form. The remains of stucco on the surface suggest that the image was once painted and covered in feathers. In its original appearance, the figure may have been more like the elaborately costumed gods as they appeared in Aztec manuscript painting. For some human sacrifices, the victim was dressed up to look like the god for whom his life was to be taken. Perhaps this piece is a representation of such a sacrificial victim.

Jaguar Cuauhxicalli, Museum of Anthropology, Mexico City. Photo: Luidger

One of the most spectacular of the surviving Aztec sculptures is a Jaguar Cuauhxicalli, a vessel to hold the hearts of sacrificial victims. The Jaguar represents the earth receiving offerings, and jaguar skins were part of the ceremonial dress of Aztec kings. Thus the animal came to symbolize the royalty. Inside the vessel on the Jaguar's back, two skeletal figures are represented in the act of bloodletting from their ears. It is thought that this sculpture, dating from the reign of Montezuma II, was intended to symbolize the links between his era and the gods of the past. Again, the simple rounded forms and powerful abstract head and mane of the Jaguar are not likely to have been quite so clear when this sculpture was in use as a receptacle for bloody sacrificial hearts.

Double-headed Serprent Pectoral, British Museum London

The Aztec craftsmen were adept at carving precious hard stone. From the southern part of the empire the Aztecs received tribute in the form of jade, porphyry and obsidian. From these stones they created colorful jewelry for the adornment of priests and the palace elite. The double-headed serpent pendant was created by applying turquoise inlays to a wood base. The red highlights of the serpents head are colored shells. This item of adornment represents the twin serpents associated with the feathered serpent god Quetzlcoatl. As fate would have it, Quetzlcoatl is the best known of the Aztec gods today, due to the fact that it featured prominently in the story of the Spanish conquest of the Aztecs.

Chapter 6: The Spanish Conquest

Hernan Cortes

Hernán Cortés, the conqueror of Mexico, like his fellow conquistadors, was an opportunist. Not waiting for orders from his superior, Velázquez de Cuéllar, Governor of Cuba, he surreptitiously set sail from Havana to enrich himself with the gold of the new world.

With a flotilla of about 11 ships, he explored the Yucatan and then moved on to Tabasco, where he fought and quickly defeated the natives. Included in the tribute he demanded of the vanquished were some 20 young native women. One of them, called La Malinche, was fluent in Maya and the Aztec language, Nahuatl. She would serve as his translator as he rampaged over Mexico, eventually becoming his mistress and the mother of his child, Martin.

Cortés sailed up the east coast of Mexico and assumed absolute control over the Spanish outpost at Veracruz. In this grab for authority over Mexico, he separated himself from the command of the Governor of Cuba and placed himself under the direct command of King Charles V. Having learned of a rich kingdom in the interior, Cortés burned his ships to make retreat impossible and set off with 500 men, a few cavalry and 15 cannons. On the way into the interior, Cortés fought and negotiated alliances with tribes he encountered. Among them were the Tlaxcalteca, who supplied some 3,000 mercenaries to the expeditionary force. Understandably, the Aztecs had many enemies in the area as a result of their own conquests, and across much of Mexico, the Spanish were viewed as liberators, not conquerors.

After arriving in the Valley of Mexico, Cortés attacked the large city of Cholula, massacred many of its 100,000 inhabitants, and burned it down, destroying perhaps as many as 365 temples. He then marched to the Aztec city of Tenochtitlan, impressively situated on an island in Lake Texcoco. When his men arrived at the lakeshore they were astounded at the sight. Much later one of Cortés' soldiers, Bernal Diaz del Castillo, wrote, "We saw so many cities and villages built both on the water and on dry land, and a straight, level causeway (to Tenochtitlan), we couldn't resist our admiration. It was like the enchantments in the book of Amadis (de Gaula, a popular Spanish chivalric romance of the late middle ages), because of the high towers, pyramids and other buildings, all of masonry, which rose from the water. Some of our soldiers asked if what we saw was not a dream."

Cortes was greeted by emissaries of the Aztec king, Montezuma II and invited to enter his great city of Tenochtitlan. Whether Montezuma was fearful of a repeat of the butchery at Cholula (as Cortés had planned) or, as was reported in the Aztec account of the event, he thought Cortés was an incarnation of the ancient Toltec god Quetzalcóatl who it was foretold would come from the east to destroy the Aztecs, the hospitality Montezuma offered to the Spanish was ill advised. The Aztec king made a second error by putting up his guests in the palace Axayácatl. Wandering about the magnificent guest quarters, the conquistadors discovered a room full of treasure. With their appetite whetted by this sight, they began to spoil for conflict.

The eager conquistadors soon found their excuse when they interrupted an Aztec religious ceremony, and, appalled by the sight of human sacrifice, massacred the Aztecs in the main temple of Tenochtitlan. In the subsequent riot, Montezuma who, by this time was being held hostage by the Spanish, was paraded before his subjects to quell the unrest. Whether he was killed by a rock thrown by one of his own people or murdered by a Spanish soldier is still unclear, but upon his death the riot turned even uglier. Cortés and his troops viciously fought their way out of Tenochtitlan and crossed a causeway to the mainland. They then laid siege to the Aztec city, cutting off the food supply. In the final attack, the conquistadors, along with their mercenary soldiers, massacred a great number of Aztecs, removed all the treasure they could put their hands on, and began to level the city.

Having subdued and destroyed Tenochtitlan, Cortés then attacked and destroyed the cities in the Valley of Mexico that had been allied with Aztecs. To top it all off, smallpox epidemics that were transferred to the natives from the Spanish wiped out an untold number even after the conquistadors left, with an estimated 10-50% of the remaining inhabitants killed. The numbers dwindled so much that the conquistadors actually merged smaller societies by forcibly transferring natives into larger population centers.

In the span of just a few years, the Aztec empire had been completely wiped out.

Chapter 7 The Aztec Legacy

Cortes and his men may have quickly conquered the Aztecs and put an end to their empire, but he never could erase their existence. The magnificence of the Aztec civilization that Cortez and his Spanish colonial followers tried so hard to obliterate from history has remained an essential part of modern Mexican identity. The current national flag of Mexico, adopted in 1984, bears the Aztec pictogram for Tenochtitlan. It shows an eagle devouring a snake perched atop a cactus with ripe prickly pears. The cactus grows on an abstract rectangular island.

The flag is one glaring reminder of the fact that Mexico City, one of the largest cities in the world, was built up out of Tenochtitlan's ashes, in a sense carrying on the Aztecs' legacy. In recognition of that fact, some of the city's landmarks and districts still have Nahuatl names, using the Aztecs' own language. Furthermore, the non-human staples of the Aztec diet continue to be prominently featured in Mexico, and now across the entire world, from maize to tortillas. Fittingly, some of these foods continue to go by their original Nahuatl names.

Beyond honoring their Aztec heritage in these ways, Mexicans are fond of celebrating their ancestral roots by dressing up as Aztecs and performing dances that are intended to recall those of their forefathers. Recreational and competitive Aztec dancing is a part of national celebration in many communities.

It is significant in the context of the evolution of modern Mexican national identity that the most important contribution to understanding Aztec civilization was inaugurated in 1978 as a huge, government sponsored project. In that year municipal workers in Mexico City by chance municipal unearthed a enormous stone disk with a relief of the dismemberment of the Aztec moon goddess. The nation was enthralled by this discovery. Thus began a major excavation of the site that has since revealed the remains of the temple precinct of Tenochtitlan and yielded thousands of artifacts that are now housed in a museum adjacent to the ruins.

That the government of Mexico spent so much of the Mexican taxpayers' money to reveal more of the city underneath the center of the modern capital is perhaps the strongest indicator that this once glorious civilization forged the foundation of a modern nation.

The Inca

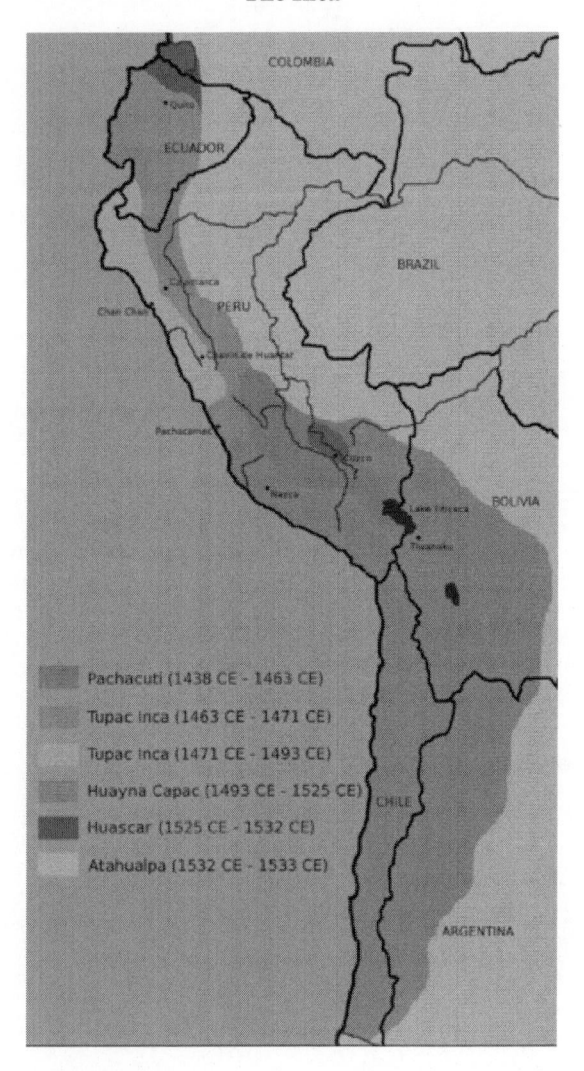

Chapter 1 History of the Incas

According to history as created by Inca oral tradition, preserved by memory keepers and written down by Spanish commentators after the conquest, there was no culture or civilization in

Peru before the Incas arrived on the scene. Given these origins, anthropologists speculate that in the interest of ensuring their dominance in the area, the Incas purposely extinguished any local histories that existed in their empire, so that for all the peoples of the empire history began when the Incas appeared. Ironically, this was accomplished in much the same way and with similar results as the Spanish attempt to destroy the Incas' own memory of their history and civilization.

Precursors of the Incas

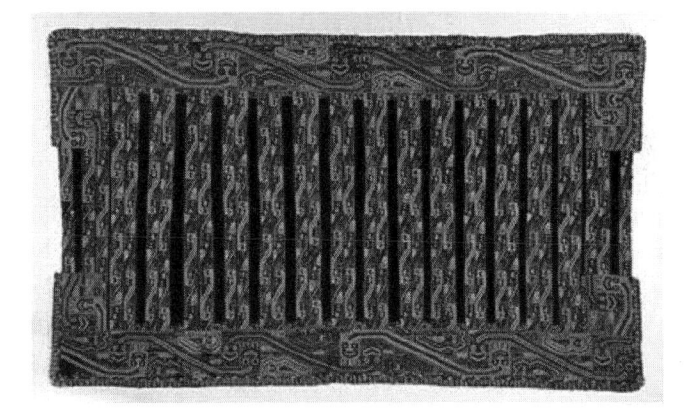

Paracas Mantle, Los Angeles County Museum of Art

The Inca people, in spite of their own propaganda or manipulated oral history, did not suddenly appear in a cultureless environment. In fact, people dwelt in the Inca lands as early as 3000 B.C., and archaeologists working at various sites have found pottery and textiles that indicate a rich history of pre-Inca Andean cultures. Among these is the Paracas culture, named by archaeologists after the Paracas Peninsula, where a rich deposit of finely woven textiles was found in shaft burials. The Paracas culture, which existed from 800-100 B.C., was based on irrigated agriculture.

Another pre-Inca culture of the region was the Moche civilization, which flourished on the coastal region of northern Peru from about 100-800 A.D. The Moche were expert builders, as the remains of their adobe temples near Huaca de la Luna testify. And around the same time the Moche were constructing their cities, the Nazca culture rose on the southern coast of Peru. It was the Nazca who etched the mysterious lines in the desert gravel around 500 A.D. that have been interpreted by UFO-ologists and New Agers to be sophisticated Martian landing strips.

One of the most advanced pre-Inca cultures was the Tiwanaku. The remains of this culture, which was centered in northern Bolivia, indicate that it was based on sophisticated agricultural practices with terraced fields and irrigated lowlands, and that it expanded its influence through widespread conquest.

Tiwanaku Vase, Tiwanaka Museum, La Paz, Bolivia Photo: Christophe Meneboeuf

It was into this rich cultural environment that the Incas inserted their own social organization and became dominant through wars of expansion and, it is assumed, astute bureaucratic control.

The Inca Story of Their Origin

The Inca myth of their origin was kept alive and modified according to their needs through oral history. They believed that their ancestors came from Pacariqtambo, about 21 miles from modern Cuzco. Here there were three caves. From the central cave came four brothers and four sisters, and from the side caves streamed the people who were to be the ancestors of all the clans of the Incas.

This group then set off to find a permanent home, but among these original leaders, only Ayar Manco of the brothers survived. The four sisters were more fortunate and all lived to help establish the first Inca city. One of the sisters, Mama Huaca, delivered Ayar Manco's son, who was called Sinchi Roca. When the migrating clans arrived in the valley of Cuzco, Mama Huaca proved herself to be a ferocious combatant against the people that the Incas found there. Using her bola (Spanish) or as it was called by the Inca, ayllo, she captured one of the enemy soldiers and ripped out his lungs and squeezed them until they exploded, thus causing the enemy to flee. Ayar Manco, or as he styled himself, Manco Cápac, and his sisters then built houses in the valley and established a town for the three original, Inca lineages.

Later History of the Inca

At Cuzco the Incas thrived under a series of rulers and under the protection of the sun god, for whom they built a temple. In the 13th century, the 8th Inca leader, Virachocha Inca, assumed the title of Sapa Inca, or unique, supreme leader. It was under his rule that the Incas began the creation of their empire by dominating the highlands around Cuzco and subjugating temporarily the Chanca people in the south of modern Peru.

In 1438, the Incas continued expanding their sphere of influence under the leadership of Pachacúti Inca Yupanqui, who after his initial conquest (or possibly re-conquest) of the Chanca placed the Inca warriors under his brother Capac Yupanqui. Unfortunately, Capac Yupanqui was unsuccessful in chasing down and slaughtering all the Chanca and was punished for his failure by forfeiting his life.

The next great expansion of the Inca Empire took place under Túpac Inca Yupanqui. As a prince commander he extended the Inca Empire north into modern Ecuador, where he rebuilt the city of Quito. After ascending to the throne in about 1471, according to a Spanish commentator, he sailed out to some islands in the Pacific, which may have been the Galapagos and Easter Island, ultimately returning to Cuzco with black people, gold and a chair of brass. This may be an entirely mythic voyage, but it is a fact that Túpac Inca Yupanqui was successful in pushing the frontiers of empire north into Ecuador and south into Chile.

The son of Túpac Inca Yupanqui was Huyana Capac who expanded the Inca Empire into Argentina and further into Chile. The Empire was now at its greatest extent, stretching over vast tracts of land in modern day Bolivia, Ecuador, Columbia, Peru, Chile and Argentina. It is thought that Huyana Capac died of smallpox, which by now was spreading rapidly from Spanish dominated Central America. It was Huyana Capac's two sons, Húascar and Atahualpa, who became engaged in civil war just prior to the arrival of the Spanish.

Chapter 2: Religion of the Incas

Although the Inca's oral traditions suggested that the history of the region began with their empire, the various gods and the religious ceremonies of the peoples that inhabited the Inca's lands before their arrival were assimilated into the Inca Empire and were incorporated into Inca religion. However, under Inca rule, all those gods were to be subordinate to those gods of the Incas themselves, so as to ensure that Imperial authority was clear and without dispute among all quarters of the Empire.

Viracocha was the primary god in the Inca pantheon. He was the origin and creator of all things. His son, the god Inti, or the sun, was married to Mama Quilla, the moon, who was also created by Viracocha. According to one myth, Inti was the father of Manco Cápac, the founder of the Inca ruling dynasty, but it was believed by some that Viracocha himself fathered Manco Cápac. In practice, the Inca centered their religious worship on Inti, and this god's High Priest was the second most important person in Inca society. The god Inti was honored at an annual celebration held each June. The Inti Raymi festival included sacrifices, feasts and sexual abstinence.

Inti, or the Sun God. Design for a flag of Peru designed by José Bernardo de Tagle, 1822

The Inca cosmology was imposed throughout the Empire, and temples to the Sun were constructed and staffed by religious officials who were allotted farmland called 'lands of the Sun'. Other local cults were provided with produce from these lands as well.

The main temple of Inca religion was the Coricancha or Sun Temple in Cuzco, in which was kept the great golden disk of the sun. The disk was appropriated by the Spanish in 1571 and sent off to the Pope. While it has disappeared, perhaps lost somewhere during the tortuous route to Spain, it remains alive in the fabulous world of adventure story writers, New Age mystics and manufacturers of souvenirs. It became a major element in the iconography of the 19th century independence movement in South America, as a symbol of nations freed from the yoke of the Spanish crown.

Two other gold images were installed in the Coricancha by Pachacúti Inca in the 15th century. One was called Viracocha Pachayachachi, which represented the creator of everything, and the other, Chuqui ylla, represented the God of Thunder. It was to Thunder that the Incas addressed their petitions for water, and shrines to him were built around the Empire, some surviving to this day in the highlands where his worship was associated with the morning star, Venus.

The moon goddess, Mama Quilla, was connected with the ruler's consort. She regulated the months and the calendar and, as such, was an important element in the creation of the Inca calendar of festivals. Her shrines were ornamented in silver and managed by priestesses.

Another female deity was Pachamama or Mother Earth. Her special interest was agriculture, and she too was of particular importance in the domain of the ruler's consort.

Chapter 3: Everyday Life among the Incas

The Incas spoke a language they called runasimi, and which the conquistadors called quechua. Quechua was introduced in the Inca culture after 1338, so it is assumed that they had another language prior to settling in Cuzco. It is also believed that the elite may have continued to use this original language. Quechua, which has eight figures of speech, no articles, no gender and a small vocabulary, was imposed as the *lingua franca* by the Incas in their empire to facilitate communication between many different cultural groups that fell under Inca administration.

The group of indigenous Andeans that established themselves as the Incas at Cuzco developed a culture that was in some ways unique and in other ways similar to that of other indigenous Andean peoples. Like all good imperialists, the Inca were expert assimilationists, making it often difficult to determine with certainty what the Inca inherited from earlier cultures and what was unique to them. For example, many of the basic ideas in their building projects had reached particularly high levels of development before the Incas employed them. Vertical archipelago agriculture practiced by the Incas, in which terraced fields were layered on mountainsides, and the construction of bridges, roads and irrigation canals, were common in Andean cultures long before the rise of the Incas.

Vertical Archipelago Agriculture, Choquequirao Peru

The Incas, however, seem to have taken the management of water to a new level of sophistication. Because cleanliness was of importance to the members of the ruling class, they included sunken baths, with hot and cold water, in their palaces. For those of minor rank in Cuzco, there were public baths in the form of fountains beside the main streets.

Given this sophistication, it is no surprise that the majority of Incas were farmers who tilled land granted to them by the ruler of the Inca state. In return for the land, the Inca farmer was required to contribute his labor to public works, and surplus food was contributed to supply the elite. The system of taxes in kind or labor was called mit'a, and it was at the very centre of the Inca social system. Of course, this arrangement was nearly identical to European feudalism of the same time period, and as it turned out, the Spanish would largely leave the mit'a system in place after conquering the Inca Empire.

Inca Clothing

Inca Tunic, Dumbarton Oaks, Washington

The nobility had a large wardrobe and changed their clothes after bathing. The males wore simple garments of rectangles of woven, naturally died alpaca or vicuña wool, which was sewn together and tied by a knot or pin. Clothes were standardized, and rank was denoted by headwear and style of hair, which was cut with obsidian knives. Sandals had soles of Llama leather and were fastened with braided cords.

Inca women's clothes were a little more complicated than those worn by the men. A long shift of two rectangles of cloth was cinched at the waist by a belt, and a second mantle which fell from shoulders to feet, closed by pins of gold and silver, was worn over it.

Both the male and female members of the nobility wore jewelry, but most was worn by men. Cylindrical ear-plugs of gold or wood were worn by the men of the royal lineage, the elite wore necklaces with metal disks, and the highest level of the aristocracy decorated themselves with wide gold and silver bracelets. Feathers were frequently used for ornamentation.

Diet

The Inca diet was very basic, consisting mostly of maize, potatoes and qunoa, while the little meat that was consumed consisted of guinea pig. All the dishes were prepared by boiling or roasting in clay ovens, since their ceramic cooking vessels were not suitable for frying.

The Inca elite seem to have supplemented their diet with some game and even fish that were brought in from the coast by runners. The drink consumed by all classes was chichi, a concoction made by chewing quinoa, maize or mollberries and spitting it into warm water, where it fermented. Very simple drinking vessels, called qero, made from wood or pottery, was used for the beverage, which was consumed in quantity at banquets and religious festivals.

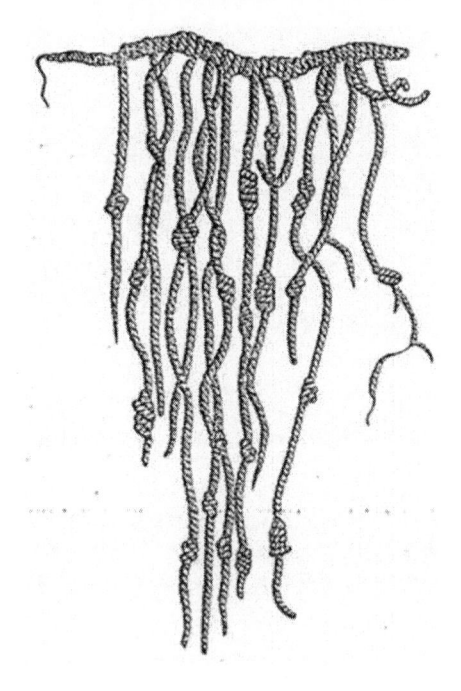

It is widely believed that Inca festivals were venues where the tales of the history of the people were retold by a special group of the elite who were responsible for keeping Imperial history. The oral records of the Inca, who had no writing, were memorized and repeated with the assistance of quipu or knotted colored cords. How exactly the quipu functioned is unknown, but it is assumed that the knots provided numerical information, which may have been in a decimal system that was decipherable by quipucamayocs or keepers of the quipus. Given their limited language and lack of writing, it's astounding that the Inca Empire was as well organized and expansive as it was, and it seems that its success can be attributed to the quipus, which were used not only for history but also for the details of administration of the empire. Amazingly, quantities of quipus found in burial sites have provided modern archaeologists and cryptographers with a puzzle which has, in spite of the application of modern code-solving techniques, yet to be solved.

As well as the recitation of history, the festivals included the presentation of drama, the singing of hymns, and the presentation of narrative poems. The hymns of Pachacuti Inca Yupanqui are among the great works of sacred poetry. One of them runs;

>O Creator, root of all,
>
>Wiracocha, end of all,
>
>Lord in shining garments
>
>Who infuses life
>
>And sets all things in order,
>
>Saying,
>
>"Let there be man!
>
>Let there ber woman
>
>Molder, maker,
>
>To all things you have given life:
>
>Watch over them,
>
>Keep them living prosperously,
>
>Fortunately,
>
>In safety and peace.

The festival actors who presented stories of heroic exploits, wars and greatness of the Incas were members of the elite - nobles, imperial administrators and priests. It is possible that the plays were accompanied by dances and music, which would have been produced by simple instruments such as flutes, drums, panpipes and conch shell horns.

Chapter 4: The Inca Empire

The Inca referred to their own empire as *Tawantinsuyu*, which meant "fourt parts together" in their language. This is because the Inca Empire was administered as four provincial departments: Chinchasuyu (NW), Antiwuyu (NE), Kuntisuyu (SW), and Qullasuyu (SE). These *Tawantinsuyu* or four regions or the four united provinces were connected to Cuzco by roads along which runners could pass quickly to deliver information from the court of the ruler to provincial governors and vice versa. The roads also allowed the quick movement of warriors to any part of the empire where they were needed, and it accomodated the large parties of those rendering mit'a or labor to make their way to construction sites, which were especially numerous in the last years of the empire.

The extent of the Inca road system is evidence of its importance in the economy and administration of the Empire. The backbone of the system of communication was the Qhapaq Ñan, which ran 3,700 miles along the length of the Andes, connecting Santiago to Quito. Many other roads allowed for the quick negotiation of the often very mountainous terrain of the empire, which encompassed a large part of western South America from southern Ecuador and Columbia and western Bolivia to northwest Argentina, and central Chile. It is estimated that the network of Inca roads totaled some 24,000 miles. With that said, the use of the word "road" is a bit of a misnomer, because the Inca had no wheeled vehicles and no pack animals. Since they always moved on foot, certain stretches of a road could more aptly be described as a narrow path.

The Imperial population connected by the road system is estimated to have been anywhere from 4 to 37 million. It is presumed that many of the quipu that have been preserved up to the present day are census records, but in the absence of a key to their code it is not possible to know with any degree of accuracy the population of the Inca Empire.

The Inca ruler, who claimed direct descent from the sun through the founder Manco Capac, considered the people of the empire his sons and all the women his spouses. His authority was spread throughout the empire by his court of elite nobles who received their power by direct connection to the ruler through royal blood.

The Inca developed a sophisticated system of imperial administration that is not yet completely understood. In the conquered territories, they apparently used the heads of the leading local families as administrators. These chiefs were called *curaca* under the Incas, and the office was hereditary. At the same time, these local administrators were not to call themselves Incas and were clearly kept in a subservient position to the elite of Cuzco. The *curaca* were responsible for ensuring that appropriate tribute was forwarded to the Inca Emperor, mainly in the form of mit'a or labor. To ensure that Imperial authority remained consistent, the children of the *curaca* were sent to Cuzco to be taught Inca administrative systems.

Not much is known about the Inca system of law and its application to the conquered territories. Presumably there were local courts that enforced edicts from Cuzco and ensured that surpluses in agricultural produce were stored and forwarded to the elite when demanded.

Chapter 5: Inca Architecture

An Inca Wall, Cuzco

Nearly 500 years after the Spanish conquest, travellers to Peru and neighboring countries that formed the Inca Empire are still amazed by the unequalled skill of Inca masons. This includes modern tourists, 19th century explorers like Hiram Bingham (the discoverer of Machu Picchu in 1911), and the Spanish conquistadors and colonial settlers.

Once again, the success of Inca architecture was a byproduct of their ability to assimilate the work and techniques of past cultures. The exacting masonry of Inca municipal buildings, paved roads, bridges, irrigation canals and agricultural terraces was not unprecedented in the region. The Incas assimilated and developed techniques of art and architecture that were already practiced in the cultures that they conquered and incorporated into their Empire.

Gate of the Sun, Tiwanaku, Bolivia

The Inca ruler Packakuti Inca Yupanqui, in his expansionist conquests, defeated the people of Tiwanaku in western Bolivia around 1450. The city he vanquished was a substantial one in which the buildings were constructed of precisely cut stone, smoothly polished and assembled in interlocking courses or layers. Tiwanaku was not a minor country outpost; archaeologists and historians speculate it may have had upwards of 285,000-1,500,000 inhabitants and controlled a large empire that it had apparently acquired over several centuries.

Walls of The Temple Kalasasaya, Tiwanaku, Bolivia. Photo: Anakin

Pakakuti was certainly impressed by the substantial glory of Tiwanaku, and as part of the tribute mit'a, he took masons to Cuzco and set them to work transforming the inferior adobe village into a highly organized symbol of power, constructed with stone. The new city was planned on the shape of a puma, which was inserted between the two rivers Huatanay and Tullumayo. Canals were then built with masonry walls to protect the city from flooding. A grid plan with narrow streets was established and plazas were laid out, with the city's blocks lined with kancha or compounds of buildings surrounded by masonry walls. The city at its greatest extent housed more than 40,000 inhabitants, and with suburban settlements was estimated by a commentator in 1553 to have had a population of 200,000.

At one end of the city - the puma's tail - was the Coricancha or Temple of the Sun. It must have been quite a sight, even if one discounts the Spanish chroniclers' propensity for exaggeration. The magnificence of this enclosed religious precinct served as a powerful symbol of Inca Imperial authority, and it was said that the Coricancha had walls and floors covered with sheets of gold and that the adjoining courtyard was full of golden statues. Unfortunately, the temple and its splendor naturally became the focus of Spanish attempts to abolish idolatry in their new empire, leading the new rulers to strip the Temple of its gold leaf interior and melt down the golden statues. Eventually, the Temple itself was levelled and replaced by the Church of Santo Domingo.

Inca Masonry Photo: Hakan Svensson

Two grand municipal plazas were laid out in the middle of Cuzco. One of these, Haucaypata Plaza, was surrounded with buildings of symbolic importance, including the temples and great halls for ceremonial and administrative gatherings.

The doorways of all these buildings were trapezoidal and had double stepped jambs. This particular architectural motif became so ubiquitous in Inca building that it appeared throughout the Empire as a symbol of the dominance of the Incas of Cuzco.

Typical Inca Doorway Ollantaytambo Photo Stevage

The administration of the Inca Empire was such that the forms of buildings and town planning established at Cuzco in the 1450's was repeated in a standardized form in building campaigns elsewhere up until the Spanish conquest. This was not unlike the municipal building programs that the British would establish through their empire. The idea that Cuzco was the center of an Empire that was comprised of four provinces was manifest in the planning of the city, where there was a central intersection of the four roads that led to the four divisions of the Empire.

Granaries or houses on hillside at Ollantaytambo

Archaeologists have studied a number of cities and towns built by the Inca's in various reaches of the Empire. In the Peruvian town of Ollantaytambo, the Incas repeated their grid plan in organizing the urban architecture, even though it stretches over uneven ground. They also repeated the form of building that was developed at Cuzco, with large and small rectangular spaces of a single story roofed with thatch supported on a wooden framework. This town, unfinished at the time of the Spanish conquest, was linked to Machu Picchu by a stone paved road. On a steep mountainside adjacent to the city there are remains of several houses or grain storage chambers clustered together. The rectangular rooms would have been covered by thatched roofs supported on a ridge pole running between the stone gabled ends.

Machu Picchu

Machu Picchu, now the best known of Inca urban centers, is a fortified city whose function in Inca civilization is still not clear. Some have speculated that it was an outpost or a frontier citadel, while others believe it to be a sanctuary or a work center for women. Still others suggest that it was a ceremonial center or perhaps even the last refuge of the Incas after the conquest. One of the theories that has taken hold is that Macchu Picchu was the summer dwelling of the Inca's royal court, the Inca's version of Versailles. As was the case with the renaming of Mayan and Aztec ruins, the names given to various structures by archaeologists are purely imaginary and thus not very helpful; for example, the mausoleum, palace or watchtower may have been nothing of the sort.

Machu Picchu Photo: Martin St.-Amant

What is clear at Machu Picchu is that the urban plan and the building techniques employed followed those at Cuzco. The location of plazas and the clever use of the irregularities in the land, along with the highly developed aesthetic involved in masonry work, follow the model of the Inca capital. The typical Incan technique of meticulous assembling ashlar masonry and creating walls of blocks without a binding material is astounding. The blocks are sometimes evenly squared and sometimes are of varying shape. In the latter case, the very tight connection between the blocks of stone seems quite remarkable. Even more astounding than the precise stone cutting of the Incas is the method that they used for the transportation and movement on site of these enormous blocks. The Incas did not have the wheel, so all the work was accomplished using rollers and levers.

The Incas did not develop a way of creating vaults of stone, so all of their structures are thus based on simple two-dimensional geometry. Because the architectural repertoire of the Incas did not include the arch or the vault, their buildings are all one story in height, the doorways and windows are headed by flat stones and are thus limited in breadth, and the ceilings are the underside of the thatched roofs.

In all the Inca cities there were one or more kallankas or great halls. The function of these buildings is still not clear. They may have been used for festivals, audiences with administrators, barracks for soldiers or council houses. One of the greatest of these kallankas is to be found at Puno, Peru. Here the Raqchi or so-called Temple of the Wiraqocha is a great rectangular long hall that had a roof supported by a series of 11 pillars along each side of a central dividing wall which itself was penetrated by 10 doorways. 15 doorways opened to the main plaza. The walls of this structure, which measure about 300 feet in length and 80 feet in breadth, were constructed in adobe set on a stone base wall.

The So-called Temple of Wiraqocha at Puno, Peru

Chapter 6: The Spanish Conquest of the Inca Empire

Tales of a great golden city somewhere to the south in the Andes spurred the Spanish conquistador Francisco Pizarro Gonzáles (c. 1471-1541) to attempt to reach this lustrous goal. In was only on his third attempt to discover the fabled riches of the Inca Empire that Pizarro achieved his goal, and as it is said, history would never be the same

Pizarro

In 1532 Pizarro marched south from Panama into Inca territory with a force that consisted of 168 men, 1 cannon and 27 horses. As he progressed, he recruited disaffected indigenous people who were apparently happy to join an expedition against their Inca overlords.

Pizzaro's army first engaged in battle with the Andean natives who were subjects of the Incas on the island of Puná (near Guayaquil, Equador). He handily routed them and establish a garrison at there. While engaged in solidifying his position Pizzaro's cohort, Hernado de Soto, returned from an expedition into the interior and reported that the King of the Incas, Atahualpa, wished to meet Pizarro. A consummate opportunist, like all successful conquistadors, Pizarro, not waiting for reinforcements, rushed off with his tiny army and a large band of native mercenaries to meet the king of the Incas.

16th century depiction of Atahualpa

    Atahualpa was resting in the city of Cajamarca (in modern-day Peru), with some 80,000 troops. He had just concluded a bloody civil war with his brother Huáscar, defeating and killing him in a battle at Quipaipan. At Cajamarca, Atahualpa was preparing to march south to the Inca capital at Cuzco and assume the Imperial throne. His fighting force may not only have been exhausted but they also may have been compromised by the arrival of smallpox that was sweeping south in advance of the Spanish incursion into the Inca Empire.

    It seems that Atahualpa was lulled into confidence because he had been told that the strangers that had recently arrived in his Empire to the north were un-menacing because they were so small in number. He let the interlopers come to him and prepared for their arrival by evacuating his warriors from Cajamarca and camping on a hill nearby. When the Spanish arrived they found an empty city. Pizarro and his troops hid in a building off the main plaza and then invited Atahualpa to come meet him. The Inca ruler, with some five or six thousand men armed with stone-age weapons such as wooden clubs and obsidian bladed spears, reentered their city.

    According to the story, as it was recorded later, Pizarro sent a Franciscan friar and a translator out to meet Atahualpa. The friar handed the Inca ruler a Bible and confidently informed him that he was now to submit to the authority of the Christian God. Atahualpa threw the Bible on the ground as a sign of his refusal to acknowledge the authority of the strange men and their divinity. Pizarro then sprung his ambush. His handful of armored, sword wielding and musket bearing troops rushed out into the plaza, cut down the guard of nobles surrounding Atahualpa and captured the Inca ruler.

Atahualpa Holding the Bible from an illustration in La Conquista del Peru (Seville, 1534).

Pizzaro, anxious to acquire the treasure he had struggled through the South American highlands to get, demanded a ransom for Atahualpa. The Incas were ordered to bring sufficient gold to fill the captured king's cell and twice that amount in silver. The volume of treasure may have been enormous if one believes that a ransom room shown to tourists today in Cajamarca was the actual place of Atahualpa's imprisonment. The Incas complied with Pizarro's demand, but the conquistador reneged on his agreement, claiming on trumped up charges that Atahualpa had murdered his brother, practiced idolatry and attempted to revolt against the Spanish. Instead, Pizarro condemned him first to be baptized, then strangled and incinerated. This was particularly galling to the Inca, who believed that the burning of their bodies or corpses would prevent them from entering the afterlife.

Portrait depicting the death of Atahualpa, the last Sapa Inca.

Having decapitated the Inca Empire with Atahualpa's death, Pizarro then marched south on the capital of Cuzco where he resumed the butchery executing many of the Inca administrative elite. The Dominican friar Bartolomé de Las Casas (c. 1484-1566),who had first-hand experience with the actions of the Spanish conquistadors in Mexico, damned Francisco Pizarro Gonzáles for his cruelty in destroying the Empire of the Incas. In his *Short Account of the Destruction of the Indies,* of 1542, Las Casas described Pizarro's violent rampage in search of gold, writing that he "criminally murdered and plundered his way through the region, razing towns and cities to the ground and slaughtering and otherwise tormenting in the most barbaric fashion imaginable the people who lived there." As evidence of the crimes, Las Casas quoted an affidavit sworn by the Franciscan Brother Marcos de Niza, who was present at the invasion. Among many atrocities Brother Marcos wrote, "I testify that I saw with my own eyes Spaniards cutting off the hands, noses and ears of local people, both men and women, simply for the fun of it."

All did not go smoothly for the avaricious and egotistical Pizarro. He soon quarrelled with a fellow conquistador, proving the dictum that there is no honor among thieves. Pizarro and his equally rapacious colleague Diego Almagro engaged in a dispute that split the pack of conquistadors and led to battle. Pizarro's camp was victorious, and he captured Almagro, who was summarily executed. Pizzaro himself, however, reaped as he had sown. He did not live long enough to enjoy the huge amount of gold and silver that was the fruit of his brutal career in the New World. He was assassinated in Lima in 1541 by Almagro's vengeful son.

The destruction of trappings of Inca civilization by the Spanish was swift and in some ways quite thorough. They installed Atahualpa's brother Manco Inca Yupanqui as a puppet king, but he was not as cooperative as they had planned. He assembled a force of warriors and re-took Cuzco in 1536 but, unable to hold the city, was forced to flee into the mountains. The Spanish periodically sallied forth into the interior to engage the remaining Incas, and in 1572 captured their last stronghold and executed Túpac Amaru, who they convinced themselves was to be the last Inca king. To further the abolition of Inca culture the Spanish terminated the Inca celebration of the Inti Raymi. The cities of the Empire were destroyed, the agriculture of the Inca civilization was wrecked and the Spanish sent the Andeans to toil in the gold and silver mines where they were literally worked to death. The decimation through war and enslavement of the Incas was furthered by visitations of European diseases including as well as smallpox, typhus, influenza, diphtheria and measles.

Depiction of Túpac Amaru, the last Inca king and namesake of rapper Tupac Shakur.

Chapter 7: The Survival of the Inca

As one would expect from a great and powerful civilization, many aspects of the Inca culture survived the depredations of the Spanish. The revolt of Manco Inca immediately after the Spanish occupation of Cuzco was not the last of Inca uprisings. In the 18th century, John Santos Atahualpa, who claimed descent from the Inca ruler murdered by the Spanish more than a century before, assembled a large force of warriors and overthrew Spanish authority in the jungles of Peru, establishing an independent territory from which the Franciscans were expelled. Eventually the Spanish managed to re-establish control over the secessionist territory.

Another bloody revolt led by Túpac Amaru II in the 18th century was put down with great difficulty by the Spanish army. Túpac Amaru II was taken with his family to Cuzco in 1780 where, after being forced to witness the execution of his wife and members of his family, he was taken to the main plaza and cruelly tortured and beheaded, with his body also being quartered. Túpac Amaru's followers abandoned the two cities they had begun to build in the Vilcabamba Valley and fled into the jungle. There are tales that somewhere in the jungle of Peru or Bolivia the last of the Incas, called the Quechuans by some, built a city called Paititi where they hid a great store of gold. To this day adventurers, inspired by New Age beliefs, continue to search for the lost last Inca city and its hoard of gold. After Túpac Amaru's revolt the Spanish banned the use of Quechua that they had used as a vehicle for the political and religious transformation of Inca culture, yet another attempt at eradicating a culture that was proving far too hard for the Spanish to kill.

Túpac Amaru II

From the beginnings of Spanish domination in the region up until the present day, the culture of the Incas survived in one form or another. It is a testament to the strength of generations of Incas that despite the slaughter of members of the elite, the destruction and reuse of the Inca city of Cuzco (including the building of the Cathedral of Santo Domingo over an Inca temple), the intense efforts to stamp out Inca religion, and the decimation of the Inca population through disease and forced labor, the Spanish did not succeed in permanently abolishing the independent culture of native Peruvians.

Peruvian Banknote with Portrait of Garcilaso de la Vega's, 1970's

Much of what we know about the details of Inca life before and after the conquest was recorded by Garcilaso de la Vega (1539-1616) in his *Comentarios Reales de los Incas*, published in Lisbon in 1609. De la Vega was the son of a conquistador and Isabel Suarez Chimpu Ocllo, an Inca princess who was the daughter of Tupac Inca Yupanqui. How de la Vega described Inca culture was colored by his education in Spanish so that the oral traditions of his ancestors on his mother's side are recorded from the perspective of a European. This combination of Inca and Spanish traditions and customs was paralleled by the development of a religious syncretism in which Inca practices and beliefs were fused with Christian precepts.

An interesting document prepared by a notary for Juan Sicos Inca in 1632 to verify his noble heritage, and thus render him immune from being forced to labor (mit'a) for the Spanish, records a religious procession that he led through the streets of Cuzco while carrying the standard of the Virgin. Juan Sicos' costume for the parade was a combination of traditional Inca garb - strings of pearls and precious stones and two chains of gold - and the festive costume of a Spanish hidalgo - armour, a sword and dagger. Following the standard of the Virgin in the parade was a second one held by three natives dressed in the "ancient style". The iconography of the standard, a canvas painted on both sides, was entirely Inca. The combination of Christian and Inca religion continues to this day.

Not only did the Inca culture survive in a modified form in Peru, but their culture also became an important part of the mentality of Europeans in assimilating a culture that for some was much superior to their own sophisticated but flawed society. The fascination with the Incas, particularly with Inca elite and most particularly with elite females, is clear in the legends and literature of Europe. According to one tale, Sebastián Bérzeviczy, the owner of Niedzica Castle in southern Poland, went to Peru and fell in love with an Inca princess. The daughter of this union, Umina, married the nephew of the insurrectionist Inca Túpac Amaru II. This nephew inherited the sacred scrolls of the Incas, which are said to have eventually been brought to

Poland before they ultimately disappeared. Naturally, the scrolls were believed to contain details about the lost treasure of the Incas.

In France the Peruvian or Inca princess was given life by the popular writer Françoise de Graffigny in her 1747 novel *Letteres d'une Péruvienne*. In the story, the Inca princess Zilia, writing to her fiancé the Inca Aza, tells of her abduction from the Temple of the Sun by the Spanish, her rescue by French sailors and her subsequent observations of French society. De Graffigny's novel was exceedingly popular, and it was published into more than 140 editions in French and other languages over the next century. Madame De Graffigny said that she was inspired to begin research on her novel by reading Garcilaso de la Vega's book after attending a performance of Voltaire's play *Alzire*. First performed in Paris in 1736, Voltaire's play is the love story of the Inca princess Alzire. On one level Voltaire's play and De Graffigny's novel were popular because they dealt with an exotic culture that was fascinating for its abundance of gold and intermittent violence, and the French idealistically portrayed the Inca as a kind of utopian civilization. Indeed, European enthusiasm for a love story that takes place within the context of a clash of Spanish and Inca cultures has had a long life. Giuseppe Verdi composed an opera, *Alzira*, with a libretto based on Voltaire's play, which was first performed in Naples in 1845.

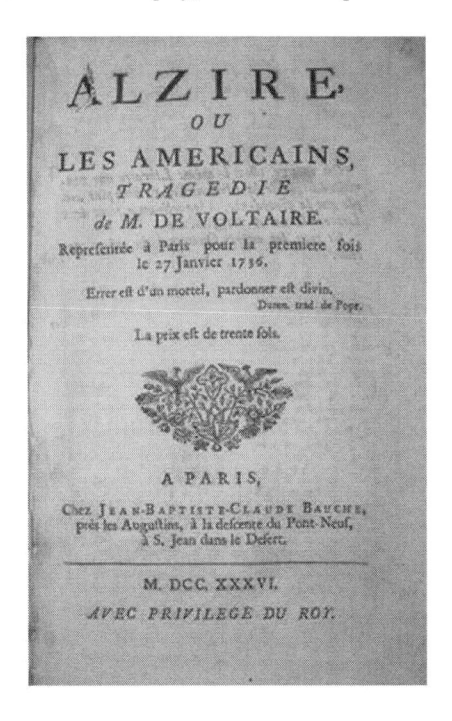

In Peru, Inca civilization has had a long life that is more prosaic than its manifestation in Europe. The declaration of independence of Peru from Spanish colonial authority in 1821 did not do much to improve the lot of the native population. In fact, the termination of the mit'a system of taxation which had continued under the Spanish and its replacement by a monetary system was detrimental to the condition of the Andean natives. Furthermore, the Inca system of land allocation without transfer of title - a kind of communal ownership of land - was replaced by systematic individual land tenure. The imposition of strict laws on the control of the land created the conditions that even today gives rise to often violent disputes with respect to mining operations. The bulk of the Andean population still struggles to maintain their culture in a system of governance that is quite foreign to them.

In the 1920's there arose a movement in Peru known as indegenismo, which sought to replace capitalist ideas of social organization with ancient Andean ones and revive the customs and traditions of the indigenous peoples. The coupling of Inca nationalism and its harkening back to a utopian world, one that has been interpreted by some intellectuals as being communal in nature, is a continuing motif in relations between the two cultures of Peru. The strongest current manifestation of indegenismo is the yearly celebration of Inti Raymi, which was revived in 1944, in which a dignitary dressed as an Inca king is paraded before a crowd of native Andeans and tourists. The ersatz Inca ruler addresses the crowd in Imperial Incan, a special form of Quechua that is still understood by some 2.5 million speakers of the language. The festival involves a number of actors and dancers following a script that was developed from the writings of Garcilaso de la Vega.

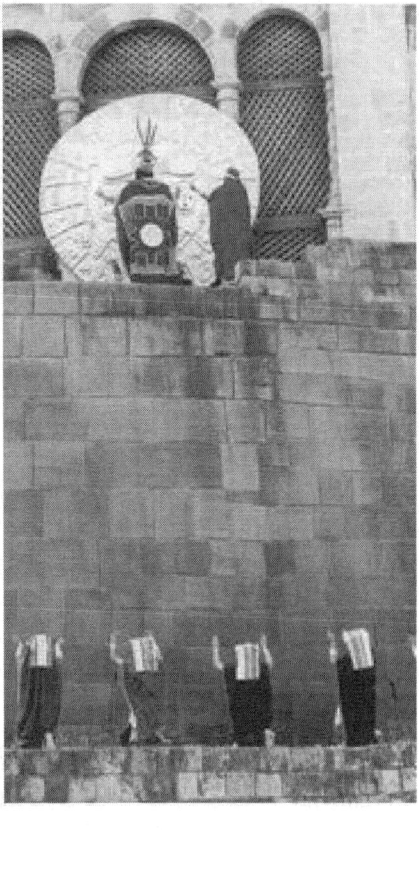

Pictures of Inti Raymi Festival (Festival of the Sun) at Sacsayhuaman, Cusco. Photos by Cyntia Motta

While the Incas in Peru continue to evolve into a society that can in some way serve to ameliorate the prejudices of history and ensure that the goals of indegenismo are considered in the evolution of the modern Peruvian state, the rest of the world remains entranced by real and imaginary tales of Inca gold and the story of the Spanish conquest. The success of Paul Shaffer's play *The Royal Hunt of the Sun*, performed in England in 1964 and subsequently on Broadway, is an example of this fascination. Schaffer's drama, which tells of Pizarro's greed and Atahualpa's agony, was made into a film in 1969, represented as an opera in 2006 and revived on the English stage in 2006.

Between the popular depictions of the Inca on both sides of the Atlantic, and the ongoing mystery over their great cities and ruins, one of the few things that can be said with certainty about the Inca is that their civilization and empire will continue to fascinate the world well into the future.

Printed in Great Britain
by Amazon.co.uk, Ltd.,
Marston Gate.